* CHINESE * DESSERT, DIM SUM & SNACK COOKBOOK

Wonona W. Chang

Irving B. Chang

Austin H. Kutscher

Lillian G. Kutscher

Sterling Publishing Co., Inc.   New York

This book is dedicated with love and gratitude to my parents, Wong Ming-Shien and Wong Chi-Niang. They nurtured and enhanced my appreciation and enjoyment of everything in life that can fill the mind, heart, and spirit with beauty and value.

W.W.C.

EDITED BY VILMA LIACOURAS CHANTILES

Library of Congress Cataloging-in-Publication Data
Main entry under title:

Chinese dessert, dim sum & snack cookbook.

    Includes index.
    1. Desserts.   2. Cookery, Chinese.   I. Chang,
Wonona W.   II. Title: Chinese dessert, dim sum and
snack cookbook.
TX773.C523 1986   641.8'6   85-26225
ISBN 0-8069-6270-4
ISBN 0-8069-6272-0 (pbk.)

Copyright © 1986 by Wonona W. Chang and Austin H. Kutscher
Published by Sterling Publishing Co., Inc.
Two Park Avenue, New York, N.Y. 10016
Distributed in Australia by Capricorn Book Co. Pty. Ltd.
Unit 5C1 Lincoln St., Lane Cove, N.S.W. 2066
Distributed in the United Kingdom by Blandford Press
Link House, West Street, Poole, Dorset BH15 1LL, England
Distributed in Canada by Oak Tree Press Ltd.
℅ Canadian Manda Group, P.O. Box 920, Station U
Toronto, Ontario, Canada M8Z 5P9
Manufactured in the United States of America
All rights reserved

Contents

Acknowledgments

As we researched, experimented, cooked, and wrote this book, many family members and friends offered encouragement, advice, time, and energy. We wish to acknowledge these efforts and express special words of thanks, appreciation and love to Mei-Ming Chang Raicer, Alan Raicer, Henriette F. Kutscher, Dr. Martin L. Kutscher, Sharon Traeger Goldberg, and Robert A. Goldberg. An extra thank-you is due Marty Kutscher for the clear photographs that will help readers on the shopping tour for some of the ingredients used in many of the recipes. We also extend our gratitude to Gloria Rocas for her assistance when we began working on this book.

We acknowledge the kindness, cooperation, and courtesy of owners and maître d's of the following restaurants that became our favorites as a result of their outstanding cuisines and the warmth and graciousness with which the food was served: Chun Cha Fu, Moon Palace, Flower Drum, Bill Hong's, Kee Wah, and HSF in New York City; and Ling's Palace in Morristown, New Jersey. In particular, we want to mention the special hospitality extended by Shu Tah Lee (Chun Cha Fu), Frank Chen and Paul Wong (Moon Palace), John Wong, K.C. Chan, and Heywood Lee (Kee Wah), Ming Ng (Bill Hong's), and John and Alice Ling (Ling's Palace).

We thank the executives of Crown Publishers, Inc. who gave their permission to adapt portions of the Guide to Ingredients, and Tea—the Everlasting Refreshment from our earlier book, *The Encyclopedia of Chinese Food and Cooking* by W.W. Chang, I.B. Chang, H.W. Kutscher, and A.H. Kutscher. New York: Crown Publishers, Inc., 1970.

Much of the symbolism and lore associated with Chinese cuisine and table elegance were imparted by C.S. Chan and Barbara Bonanno of the Wing Fat Oriental Art Store, Atlantic City, New Jersey.

A final note is added—in loving remembrance of the late Helene W. Kutscher who, more than twenty years ago, initiated the friendship and scholarly efforts that inspired this work's authors to pursue the quest for quality in all dimensions of life.

W.W.C.
I.B.C.
A.H.K.
L.G.K.

Introduction

Chinese restaurants in the United States offer few authentic Chinese desserts or American adaptations of Chinese desserts. Restaurant menus list only a limited number of fairly prosaic desserts. Generally, these include pineapple chunks, fortune cookies, almond cookies, ice cream, fresh available fruit, and occasionally, a serving of canned or preserved lychees or kumquats.

Likewise, the dessert recipes in English-language Chinese cookbooks are limited in number and variety. In a survey of more than 35 cookbooks in print, we found the expected paucity in the number of dessert recipes—a paucity that became more impressive considering the ratio of dessert recipes to entrée recipes, approximately a dozen of the former to *hundreds* of the latter. Further confirming this imbalance is the allotment of pages for "desserts"—two and one half pages—compared with the pages for "other" recipes—100 pages—for most books. Of the books we examined, which averaged 228 pages, only an average of seven and one half pages comprised the dessert sections.

These observations contrast sharply with the Western style of eating that anticipates and may include desserts, candies, and sweet snacks at mealtimes, throughout the day, and even at bedtime. No consideration has been given to those of us who would enjoy a satisfying dessert when eating out or who would enjoy testing our ingenuity, knowledge, and cooking talents by climaxing a Chinese dinner at home with a Chinese dessert. Such a dessert would add a highlight to the meal.

A logical explanation of this incongruous situation may be that in old China desserts as we know them today were usually served in the middle of the meal, followed by a steamed poultry, meat, or other dish. Many times, soup or tea alone marked the end of even a sumptuous dinner. Many Americans and Europeans, however, have not happily accepted this state of culinary affairs; their tradition literally dictates that the dessert be sweet, rich, refreshing, and often elaborately prepared and presented. A casual review of the dessert categories in the most popular and widely circulated cookbooks reveals this concept, verified by a large number of dessert cookbooks. The desserts served in French, Italian, German, and other ethnically based restaurants also reflect these rich recipes in all their glory.

In writing this book, we wish to introduce into the Chinese-International cuisine comparable sweet delights. We have carefully considered the taste buds' adaptability to esoteric ingredients and flavors and offer readers a dual challenge — to enjoy unique ingredients and to prepare and serve familiar foods in new ways. This collection of dessert recipes is the result. The recipes, on the one hand, are indigenous to China and, on the other, combine ingredients from the East and West. A very small number of pastries, compotes, custards, and other sweets will be familiar to those who have mastered Chinese cooking. For them and other readers, however, the array of desserts offered in this book will add a new dimension to the home-cooked Chinese dinner, since these desserts far exceed the number, variety, and depth of recipes currently found in any other Chinese cookbook.

Many dessert recipes in this book have been prized as family treasures for generations and are authentic; others have been adapted to the Chinese cuisine by the addition of oriental ingredients, such as fresh or preserved fruits, vegetables, and nuts, readily available in Chinese or specialized food markets and departments.

Cooking is an art. A person does not cook just to fill an empty stomach but to exercise imagination and creativity. The flexibility and ingenuity of Chinese cooking styles foster the development of these talents when new dishes and ingredients are incorporated into our menus.

DIM SUM & SNACKS

One category of food — dim sum — relates to all others in this book. Literally translated, dim sum means, "Dot the heart," but, more poetically, the words mean, "Point to your heart's desire." With their many differing tastes, textures, and fragrances, dim sum can appear on the table as snacks, desserts, and festival dishes. Dim sum are served in numerous ways: as luscious little dumplings stuffed with an assortment of savory meats; as noodles cooked in soup or stir-fried with meats and vegetables; as deliciously braised meats simmered in succulent sauces; as steamed bread filled with sweet bean paste or hearty roast pork; as combinations of beef, chicken, and vegetables; as delicate dessert pastries filled with fruit, jams, and nuts — the numbers are infinite! And you can enjoy dim sum any time of day, at mealtime or snacktime.

In China, teahouses open in the early morning hours to serve dim sum as breakfast foods or as snacks for those who have worked at night jobs. Teahouse chefs are highly creative. They invent exceptional dishes. Their customers often visit a particular teahouse or restaurant because of the wide acclaim it has received for its distinctive dishes. People gather for family, social, and business engagements at the teahouse. This book includes a varied selection of dim sum discovered in these popular establishments and a special section, Tea — the Everlasting Refreshment.

FESTIVAL DISHES & THE CHINESE NEW YEAR

Of all the festivals in the Chinese lunar calendar, Chinese New Year is the most celebrated and joyous. Along with old traditions, family fun, feasting, and joy, the Chinese people emphasize deeds that are honorable and kind.

In preparing for the festival, homes are alive with activities — cleaning every corner, cooking, baking. Special foods, different from the usual daily fare, are served. The festival fills its celebrants with appreciation for those moments in life when blessings can be counted and savored. Calligraphic symbols representing life's blessings are visible as wall decorations in Chinese communities. The most familiar of these are the Chinese characters for happiness, good health, long life, and love—blessings of the spirit.

Festivals also celebrate the material blessings that can ease the path through life. Three characters, in particular, can be found as the designs of a picture, scroll, or mural in many Chinese homes. One of these characters represents *Fu*, the opportunity to dine and delight in good food, and the first blessing: "Blessed are those who enjoy and find happiness in food." The second represents *Lu*, wealth sufficient to support material needs and personal comforts, and a second blessing: "Those who are wealthy and with high status are the ones who can afford good garments." The third represents *So*, the achievement of longevity and the fruition of a long life with inner peace and knowledge of true relaxation, and a third blessing: "Those who can relax and sleep well are the ones who will enjoy long life."

The New Year's Eve festival— *Tuan Nien*—is commemorated by a grand feast for all family members. On that evening, the children are allowed to stay up to enjoy the last hours of the old year, a custom called *Shou Swei*, literally meaning "guiding the year out," which will bring longevity to the parents, according to legend.

All the foods and fruits served and displayed at the New Year's celebration have their own special significance. Red is the dominant color for the Chinese New Year. Red symbolizes happiness and life, but many other colors are found on the table in the wide assortment of the food served.

In Mandarin, the tangerine is called "*gee*," which means good fortune. In Cantonese, it is called "*gum*," which is similar to the word for gold and hence, prosperity. The pomegranate, known as the Chinese apple, symbolizes fertility because of its many seeds. Sugar cane indicates continued success. New Year Cake represents prosperity and success. Lotus roots symbolize long life and strong family ties, the pear good prospects for the New Year, apples peace and safety. Peanuts are known as the long-life fruit. Watermelon seeds signify, "May what you say and think be harmonious and pleasant." *Wan nien liang* means "Ten thousand years of food" or "May heaven bless our food," and is represented by an evergreen twig standing upright on a tangerine which has been placed in a bowlful of uncooked rice.

At the Chinese New Year celebration, firecrackers are set off and the dragon dance is performed. While the dragon dances off to the clanging of the gong and cymbal, the beating of the drum, and the startling sound of exploding firecrackers, happiness, good health, and prosperity for the coming year are ushered in.

Although the Chinese New Year celebration may differ slightly from region to region in China and in other countries, it always remains a joyful and precious festival. Guests are served tea with sweet preserved fruit, candied water chestnuts, melon, lotus roots, or dates—all symbolizing wishes for a year filled with sweetness. Recipes throughout this book are prepared for friends and family at the time of the Chinese New Year.

BEFORE
YOU BEGIN

Conversion Guides

CUSTOMARY TERMS		METRIC SYMBOLS	
t.	teaspoon	mL	millilitre*
T.	tablespoon	L	litre
c.	cup	mg	milligram
pkg.	package	g	gram
pt.	pint	kg	kilogram
qt.	quart	mm	millimetre
oz.	ounce	cm	centimetre
lb.	pound	°C	Celsius
°F	degrees Fahrenheit		
in.	inch		

*Millilitre is also abbreviated ml.

Guide to Approximate Equivalents

CUSTOMARY				METRIC	
Ounces Pounds	Cups	Tablespoons	Teaspoons	Millilitres	Grams Kilograms
			¼ t.	1 mL	1g
			½ t.	2 mL	
			1 t.	5 mL	
			2 t.	10 mL	
½ oz.		1 T.	3 t.	15 mL	15 g
1 oz.		2 T.	6 t.	30 mL	28 g
2 oz.	¼ c.	4 T.	12 t.	60 mL	60 g
4 oz.	½ c.	8 T.	24 t.	125 mL	120 g
8 oz.	1 c.	16 T.	48 t.	250 mL	225 g
1 lb.					450 g
	4 c.			1 L	
2.2 lb.					1 kg

Keep in mind that this not an exact conversion, but generally may be used for food measurement. Also, some weights (ounces and grams) taken from manufacturers' packages may not be consistent or standard.

Equivalent Food & Cookery Terms

AMERICAN	BRITISH	AMERICAN	BRITISH
All-purpose flour	Plain flour	Ground meat	Minced meat
Bacon	Rashers	Heavy cream	Double cream
Broil	Grill	Light cream	Single cream
Brown sugar	Demerara sugar	Molasses	Treacle
Candy	Sweets; confections	Rock candy	Rock sugar
Confectioners' sugar	Icing sugar	Scallion	Spring or green onion
Cookie	Biscuit	Shrimp	Prawn
Cornstarch	Cornflour	Squid (calamari)	Inkfish
Eggplant	Aubergine	Zucchini	Baby marrow or
Fine granulated white sugar	Caster (castor) sugar		courgette

Using the Recipes

1. Before you begin having fun preparing the recipes, review the Guide to Ingredients to become familiar with food characteristics.

2. *Almost every recipe will serve four people*. If more servings are needed, double the quantities of ingredients—except for cooked dishes. For these, we advise preparing the recipes twice; doubling certain ingredients can alter the taste or cooking time.

3. There is nothing unique about any of the utensils used to cook Chinese desserts. A frying pan or saucepan (preferably coated to prevent sticking) are suitable. The nonstick coating of frying pans or saucepans also simplifies the cleanup when sugary mixtures harden onto the pan sides.

4. Leftover juices drained from canned fruits should be saved for your punches and other beverages. Juices will keep for several days if stored, covered, in the refrigerator or much longer in the freezer.

5. Where brand names have been listed for certain products, no endorsement of the product is intended. While creating and testing our recipes, these brands proved to be excellent and contributed substantially to the end product. Other brands may be substituted; when used, however, some alterations by taste may be needed in the recipes to accommodate for differences in flavor or texture. For example, Dundee ginger marmalade has a pleasantly distinctive flavor, while other ginger marmalades can taste "musty."

6. The liqueurs used in many recipes are preferred for their flavors, but alcoholic substitutes could include rum, Drambuie liqueur, anisette, fruit cordials, gin, and vodka.

7. If a sauce is supposed to be thick and it appears to be too *thin*, 1 teaspoon (5 mL) cornstarch blended into 1 tablespoon (15 mL) cold water can be slowly added by teaspoonfuls into the hot sauce, stirring constantly until the desired results are obtained. If necessary, this procedure may be repeated.

   If a sauce is too *thick*, pour it back into the saucepan and add warm water, 1 tablespoon (15 mL) at a time, stirring well until the desired results are obtained.

8. Most people are accustomed to thick and creamy puddings. Some puddings suggested in this book have a looser consistency. It is possible to thicken these puddings by adding cornstarch, but this is not fully recommended because thickening can change the flavor.

9. In dishes where jelling is necessary, or if a sugared or other coating is applied, dry the canned fruits on paper towelling before coating them.

10. We recommend refined brown sugar in recipes calling for brown sugar.

11. Most recipes for baked cakes or cookies indicate the use of margarine, not butter, as the preferred shortening.

Guide to Ingredients

Cooking and the enjoyment of food are arts that challenge our five senses. Learning the basic vocabulary of ingredients is the first step towards creating a work of culinary art. The following guide describes the ingredients traditionally and practically used in the preparation of Chinese desserts, dim sum, snacks, and festival dishes. The Chinese people consider highly important the skills of cooking and fine dining. They use their senses to combine ingredients, accenting the taste, aroma, texture, and color that enhance the aesthetic qualities of a dish. Many ingredients in this guide are uniquely Chinese; some have been adopted from other cuisines.

All ingredients in the following list have been graded by an index of importance in the Chinese cuisine, ranging from 4 down to 1. A 4 rating indicates either that the ingredient is most important or essential to a specific dish or that its widespread use makes it an absolute necessity in the Chinese cupboard. Rarely can a substitute of similar quality or flavor be found for a 4 ingredient. Ingredients rated 3 are used in many Chinese dishes and add to their authenticity. Ingredients rated 2 are used infrequently and may not be readily available. Substitutes can be found for these. Ingredients rated 1 are difficult to obtain, rarely used, or are acceptable to only the most sophisticated palates.

The transliterations follow each ingredient: (Cantonese) (Mandarin), in that order. Example: AGAR-AGAR (*dung yong tsoi* is Cantonese) (*dung yang tsai* is Mandarin).

AGAR-AGAR (*dung yong tsoi*)(*dung yang tsai*)
Type of food: vegetable (gum from seaweed)
Length: about 12 in. (30.5 cm)
Shape: flat, stringlike
Color: transparent
Surface: dry
Consistency: hard until soaked
Aroma: none
Taste: none
Uses: salad ingredient; mixed with vegetables or meat
Available forms: dried, in 4-oz. (120-g) package
Storage: in pantry, indefinitely
When available: always
Where purchased: Chinese grocery
Approximate cost: moderately expensive
Substitutes: none
Importance: 1

ARBUTUS
Type of food: fruit
Length: ¾–1 in. (19–25 mm)
Shape: round
Color: dark raspberry; maroon
Surface: tender, uniformly pebbled (only canned variety available in some countries outside China)
Consistency: fleshy, soft, and tender
Aroma: slight, similar to purple plum or lychee
Taste: fruity, delicate, fragrant, refreshing, distinctive, between raspberry and canned plum
Uses: dessert or snack; when pitted, combined with other fruit; alone, chilled in syrup; with other flavorings added (fresh grated ginger); syrup or fruit, pitted and crushed in blender, valuable in Chinese mixed fruit beverages
Available forms: only in cans, packed in syrup
Storage: in unopened can—indefinitely; removed from can, in covered container—in refrigerator for 3–5 days
When available: always
Where purchased: Chinese and Thai grocery stores
Approximate cost: moderately expensive
Substitutes: lychees, loquats, longans—in concept of refreshing and uniquely flavored fruit only
Importance: 2–3

BEAN CURD OR TOFU (DOW FOO)
Type of food: bean cake or custard
Shape: flat, square, about 3 in. × ½ in. (7.6 × 1.3 cm) thick
Color: cream; white
Consistency: only the most creamy, silky variety to be used for the recipes in this cookbook; firm, gelatinous, moist, soft, tender
Aroma: none
Taste: bland, delicate, subtle
Uses: main ingredient; may be used whole, cubed, sliced, shredded, mashed
Available forms: usually as described above and stocked in tubs or containers filled with water; also available in sealed packets; other varieties available but are

not recommended for the recipes noted here
Storage: fresh, covered with water (which should be changed every other day), in refrigerator—about 1 week
When available: always
Where purchased: Chinese (preferred), Japanese, and Korean groceries; supermarkets
Approximate cost: inexpensive
Substitutes: none
Importance: 4, in general; 3, in terms of use in dessert recipes

BEAN FILLING, SWEET (*dow sa*)(*do sa*)
Type of food: vegetable (made from kidney or mung beans)
Color: red (kidney beans), green (mung beans)
Consistency: dry, thick paste
Aroma: slight
Taste: sweet
Uses: flavoring agent; stuffing for pastry
Available form: canned
Storage: in refrigerator for several months
When available: most commonly at Chinese New Year
Where purchased: Chinese bakery or grocery
Approximate cost: inexpensive
Substitutes: date jam or sweet potatoes
Importance: 4

CABBAGE, WHITE CHINESE (*bok tsoi*)(*bai tsai*)
Type of food: vegetable
Length: 12–16 in. (40.6 cm)
Shape: leafy, long stalk
Color: white; green
Surface: dull, smooth
Consistency: crunchy, firm, moist (raw); tender, crisp (cooked)
Aroma: none
Taste: subtle, bland
Uses: main ingredient
Available forms: fresh, by the pound; dried, in ½-lb. (225-g) packages
Storage: wrapped in plastic bag or paper, in refrigerator—1 week; dried—indefinitely

When available: always (winter crop is best)
Where purchased: Chinese grocery; supermarkets
Approximate cost: inexpensive
Substitutes: lettuce
Importance: 4, in general; 2, in terms of desserts

CHESTNUTS, WATER (*ma tie*)(*ma ti*)

Type of food: fruit, root
Shape: bulbous, round, tapered
Color: brownish-purple skin, yellowish-white interior
Surface: dull
Consistency: chewy, crispy, crunchy, firm, fleshy, moist, meaty
Aroma: slight, fruity, appetizing
Taste: bland, delicate, subtle, meaty
Uses: garnish; main ingredient; stuffing; candy; thickening agent in flour form
Available forms: fresh, locally grown, by weight; canned; dried and ground into powder or flour (provides particularly desirable crispness for batter coating), imported; sugared, sold as sweetmeat at Chinese New Year
Storage: fresh, in pantry—1 week, in refrigerator—2 weeks; dried powder, in pantry—indefinitely; sugared, in jar in pantry—indefinitely
When available: always
Where purchased: fresh and canned, in Chinese grocery and supermarkets
Approximate cost: fresh and canned, inexpensive; water chestnut flour, relatively expensive
Substitutes: none
Importance: 3+

COCONUT STRIPS, CHINESE (*tong long*)(*ping tang yea tze*)

Type of food: fruit
Length: to 2 in. (5.1 cm)
Shape: ½-in. (13-mm)-wide strip
Color: white
Surface: dull, pebbly, textured
Consistency: crunchy, dry, firm, fleshy, chewy
Aroma: none
Taste: delicate, sweet

Uses: confection
Available forms: as a crystallized sweetmeat, sold by weight, usually in plastic bag
Storage: in plastic bag or covered jar in the pantry—indefinitely
When available: during and after Chinese New Year
Where purchased: Chinese grocery
Approximate cost: inexpensive
Substitutes: crystallized fruits, peels, or melons
Importance: 1

COOKIES, ALMOND (*hong young bang*)(*hsin ren bing*)

Type of food: dessert cookie
Shape: round
Color: light brown
Surface: textured
Consistency: crisp, dry
Aroma: almond
Taste: almond
Uses: dessert
Available forms: loose (in bulk by weight) or in packages or tins
Storage: in freezer or pantry, like any other cookie—for several months
When available: always
Where purchased: Chinese grocery or bakery
Approximate cost: inexpensive
Substitutes: any cookies
Importance: 4 (for children)

DATE JAM

Type of food: fruit preserve
Color: dark brown; prune-colored
Surface: smooth
Consistency: smooth, thick, stiff
Aroma: sweet, aromatic, fruity
Taste: sweet, fruity, pleasant
Uses: filling or stuffing for Chinese pastry; as a spread for English muffins or bread; topping for cookies, cakes; stuffing for dried or glacéed fruits; as sauces; eaten by itself as dessert; also as main flavoring ingredient in ice cream, sherbets or ices
Available forms: as paste/jam, in cans only
Storage: in unopened can—indefinitely; removed from can, in covered bowl in

refrigerator—for several weeks
When available: in cans, always
Where purchased: Chinese grocery
Substitutes: sweet red bean paste in some
dishes, including ice cream; cake or tart
fillings; spreads
Approximate cost: inexpensive
Importance: 4

DATES, RED, DRIED (*hung jo*)(*hung tzao*)

Type of food: fruit
Length: 1 in. (2.5 cm)
Shape: oval to round
Color: red
Surface: glossy
Consistency: dry, firm, hard, moist
interior; or if processed, a soft paste or
jam
Aroma: slight, sweet
Taste: bland, delicate, sweet
Uses: flavoring agent, garnish, stuffing for
pastry
Available forms: as a jam, in cans; dried,
in plastic packages by weight
Storage: date jam, in covered bowl in
refrigerator—for weeks; dried dates, in
tightly covered container in pantry—
indefinitely
When available: always
Where purchased: Chinese grocery
Approximate cost: jam, about the same as
any preserve; dried dates, moderately
expensive
Substitutes: none
Importance: 4 (date jam)

EGG ROLL WRAPPERS OR SKINS
(*chwin guen pei*)(*chwin jwen pi*)
Type of food: pastry
Shape: ⅛-in. (3-mm) thick, 6 in. (15.2 cm)
square
Color: fresh dough
Surface: doughy when raw; fragile when
cooked
Consistency: crisp
Aroma: none
Taste: delicate
Uses: filled with meat or fish and
vegetable mixture and deep-fried

Available forms: fresh by weight
Storage: in refrigerator—3 or 4 days;
frozen, if well wrapped to preserve
moisture—for several months (but
becomes brittle in time)
When available: always
Where purchased: Chinese grocery;
supermarkets, occasionally
Approximate cost: inexpensive
Substitutes: none
Importance: 4

FIVE SPICES POWDER (*ng hiong fun*)(*wu hsiang fun*)
Type of food: spice (star anise; Chinese
cinnamon; fennel or aniseed; Szechwan
pepper or Chinese pepper, and clove)
Color: brownish-red
Consistency: powdery
Aroma: strong, sweet, appetizing, fragrant
Taste: spicy, tangy
Uses: flavoring agent; blending agent in
sauce
Available forms: in powdered dry form in
cans
Storage: in pantry—indefinitely
When available: always
Where purchased: Chinese grocery;
occasionally in specialty food shops
Approximate cost: inexpensive
Substitutes: mixture of 1 t. (5 mL) each—
ground cinnamon, cloves, aniseed, and
thyme
Importance: 4

GINGER (Fresh) (*giong*)(*jiang*)
Type of food: root
Length: to 6 in. (15.2 cm)
Shape: irregularly bulbous, gnarled,
knobby root
Color: brownish-grey (yellow-ivory inside)
Surface: dull, indented or pocked;
textured skin or hull
Consistency: crunchy, firm, fleshy, tender
(if young); tough (if old)
Aroma: sweet, pungent
Taste: sharp, spicy, tangy
Uses: in sauce, as condiment, seasoning,
flavoring agent, medicine

Available forms: fresh roots sold loose by weight; powder, in tins; liquid essence, in bottle; pickled red, in bottle; pickled, to go with other vegetables, in cans; crystallized (sugared, candied), used as dessert or to flavor dessert, in packages; preserved in syrup, in jars; sweetened stem ginger; preserved as confection
Storage: fresh, wrapped in foil or plastic bag in vegetable compartment of refrigerator—about 2 months (avoid wetting or drying out ginger); if peeled and sliced or left in knobs, in sherry, tightly covered in jar—indefinitely; dry powder, on shelf—indefinitely; crystallized—indefinitely
When available: fresh, always; fresh new roots, only in spring
Where purchased: Chinese, Spanish, Japanese, and Korean groceries
Approximate cost: inexpensive
Substitutes: for fresh ginger: ground ginger ⅛ t. [.5 mL] is equivalent to 1 T. [15 mL] freshly grated ginger)
Importance: 4

GINGER BRANDY

Type of food: cordial, flavoring agent
Color: golden brown, light
Aroma: brandy-like with faint ginger scent
Taste: strong, sweet brandy flavor with ginger accent
Uses: as cordial; as flavoring agent in almost any fruit compote, sauce, topping, marinade, filling, or punch
Storage: in unopened bottle—indefinitely; if opened, well sealed—indefinitely
Where purchased: Chinese or other liquor stores (may have to be specially ordered)
When available: always
Approximate cost: inexpensive
Substitutes: none to duplicate ginger flavor; other fruit-flavored cordials, wines or brandies will provide acceptable, if differently flavored, substitute
Importance: 3–4

HOISIN SAUCE (Red Seasoning Sauce)

(*hoy sin joing*)(*hai hsien jiang*)
Type of food: condiment sauce, a combination of soybean flour, red beans, ginger, garlic, spices, salt, chili, and sugar

Color: brown-red
Consistency: thick fluid or thin paste
Aroma: pungent, sweet, garlic-like
Taste: beany, spicy, sweet, tangy
Uses: condiment; flavoring agent; marinating agent; dip for meats
Available forms: cans, usually 8-oz. (225-g) size
Storage: in tightly covered jar in refrigerator—indefinitely
When available: always
Where purchased: Chinese grocery
Approximate cost: inexpensive
Substitutes: duck sauce
Importance: 4

JACKFRUIT

Type of food: fruit
Length: 11 in. (27.9 cm), in natural fresh state; 2-in. (5.1-cm)-long slices, in canned variety
Shape: long and rounded at edges; canned segments are flat, ⅓ in. (8 mm) thick, 2 in. (5.1 cm) long, 1 in. (2.5 cm) wide
Color: brown skin with creamy white flesh
Surface: smooth, rough, small nodular skin, in natural fresh fruit; smooth and peeled, in canned variety
Consistency: canned variety, tougher than the lychee; of same consistency as rambutan; fleshy; pitted
Aroma: very fragrant when ripe and fresh; slightly sweet and fruity
Taste: bland
Uses: as dessert
Available forms: only in can or jar; not available as fresh fruit
Storage: if unopened—indefinitely; removed from can, in syrup in covered container in refrigerator—3–5 days
When available: in can, always
Where purchased: Chinese grocery shops only (but not always)
Approximate cost: moderately expensive
Substitutes: none
Importance: 1 (due to lack of availability)

KIWI

Type of food: fruit
Length: 2–3 in. (5.1–7.6 cm)
Shape: rounded oval, nearly symmetrical
Color: medium-dark greyish-green skin;

dark green with many small black seeds inside (edible, like banana seeds)
Surface: smooth peel, covered with fine hairs; interior surface, shiny and glossy
Consistency: fleshy, delicate, soft, tender
Aroma: odd when cut, slightly pungent with own distinctive fruity scent
Taste: slightly sharp, aromatic, fruity, unique
Uses: as dessert or garnish, or combined with various other flavorings and fruits
Storage: at room temperature or in refrigerator — 1 week
Available forms: only fresh
When available: most of the year
Where purchased: better fruit and grocery shops — Chinese or general
Approximate cost: moderately expensive (but a few go a long way)
Substitutes: none
Importance: 3

KUMQUAT (*gum quot*)(*jin jiu*)
Type of food: fruit
Length: to 1 in. (2.5 cm)
Shape: oval (elongated)
Color: orange
Surface: shiny, smooth
Consistency: firm, fleshy, juicy, soft (inside), seedy
Aroma: pungent, sweet, gingery
Taste: spicy, syrupy (preserved), sweet (outside), tart (inner meat)
Uses: garnish, stuffing, main ingredient, dessert
Available forms: fresh, in fruit baskets; preserved, in syrup packed in small or large jars; preserved and sugared (crystallized), loose, by weight or in smaller quantities in plastic bags
Storage: fresh, in refrigerator — about 2 weeks; preserved in syrup, in pantry or refrigerator — indefinitely; preserved and sugared, in tightly covered jar — many months; dries out after a month or 2 in plastic bags
When available: fresh, in winter; preserved in syrup, always; sugared, at time of Chinese New Year for about 2 to 3 weeks
Where purchased: fresh and preserved in syrup, in Chinese or other groceries; sugared, Chinese grocery

Approximate cost: moderately expensive
Substitutes: other very heavy syrup packed or sugared fruits (candied orange peel)
Importance: 4

LONGANS (nicknamed "dragon eye")(*loong gnahn*)(*lung yen*)
Type of food: fruit
Length: ½–1 in. (13 mm–2.5 cm)
Shape: round
Color: yellow-tan
Surface: smooth shell and interior
Consistency: fleshy, soft, tender, with pit
Aroma: slight, sweet
Taste: delicate, fragrant, refreshing, distinctive
Uses: desserts, garnish, sweet and sour dishes; dried longans are used in slow-cooked soups
Available forms: dried, shelled, pitted, and packed solidly in the form of a bar; canned, packed in syrup
Storage: dried and canned, in pantry — indefinitely
When available: always
Where purchased: Chinese grocery
Approximate cost: moderately expensive
Substitutes: raisins, lychees
Importance: 3

LOQUAT (*pei pa*)(*p'i pa*)
Type of food: fruit
Length: to 2 in. (5.1 cm)
Shape: round
Color: orange
Surface: glossy, smooth
Consistency: fleshy, tender with pit
Aroma: slight, sweet
Taste: delicate, bland
Uses: dessert
Available forms: canned, packed in syrup, about 8–20-oz. (227–565-g) cans; fresh, rarely found in Western countries; preserved, dried in boxes
Storage: canned, when opened, in covered container in refrigerator — several days
When available: always
Where purchased: Chinese grocery
Approximate cost: moderately expensive
Substitutes: lychees or longans
Importance: 3

LOTUS ROOT (*leen gnow*)(*lien ngo*)
Type of food: vegetable root
Length: to 8 in. (20.3 cm)
Shape: 4 × 8-in. (10.2 × 20.3-cm) bulb growing attached and sold in a series or by individual root
Color: brown-red-tan
Surface: smooth skin or hull
Consistency: firm, chewy, crisp, crunchy
Aroma: sweet
Taste: sweet, bland, delicate
Uses: as dessert sweetmeat (when crystallized); soup ingredient, vegetarian dishes
Available forms: sugared, in plastic packages or loose by weight; fresh, by the whole bulb or segment sold by weight; dried slices; dried, powdered stem (not used in desserts)
Storage: fresh, in refrigerator vegetable crisper—2–3 weeks; sugared, will keep indefinitely in covered jar in pantry
When available: candied, at Chinese New Year and, occasionally, during the year; fresh, July to February
Where purchased: Chinese grocery
Approximate cost: moderately expensive
Substitutes: none
Importance: 3

LOTUS SEED (*leen tszee*)(*lien tze*)
Type of food: vegetable seed
Length: to ½ in. (13 mm)
Shape: ¼ × ½-in. (6 × 13-mm) seed
Color: brown
Surface: has skin or hull
Consistency: hard
Aroma: none
Taste: delicate
Uses: candy, soup flavoring agent
Available forms: canned or dried
Storage: indefinitely
When available: always
Where purchased: Chinese grocery
Approximate cost: moderately expensive to expensive
Substitutes: nonc
Importance: 1

LYCHEE (LITCHI)(*la-ee tzee*)(*li tze*)
Type of food: fruit
Length: to 1 in. (2.5 cm)

Shape: round
Color: red-purple skin or hull; interior meat is opaque or white when canned or fresh; brown when dried
Surface: pebbly, textured skin or hull; smooth interior meat
Consistency: firm, fleshy, soft, tender; dried, chewy, pitted
Aroma: slight, sweet (fresh and canned)
Taste: bland, delicate, sweet, tangy; dried, strong and sweet
Uses: flavoring agent, dessert, garnish, for sweet and sour dishes
Available forms: fresh, in bags by weight; canned, in various sizes, packed in syrup; dried, in boxes or transparent bags
Storage: fresh, in refrigerator—about 1 week; canned, in pantry—indefinitely; dried—indefinitely
When available: fresh, for about 1 month only in summer; canned, always; dried, always
Where purchased: Chinese grocery
Approximate cost: fresh, expensive; canned, moderately expensive; dried, expensive
Substitutes: loquats (canned), longans (canned)
Importance: 4

MANDARINE NAPOLÉON LIQUEUR
Type of food: cordial, flavoring agent
Color: medium dark brown
Aroma: tangerine, mandarin orange, sharply aromatic
Taste: tangy, orange; strong but sweet; definitely alcoholic
Uses: as cordial; as flavoring agent in a fruit marinade; as flavoring agent in almost any fruit compote, sauce, topping, filling, punch, or other dish
Storage: in unopened bottle—indefinitely; opened, if well sealed—indefinitely
Where purchased: general or Chinese liquor shops (may have to be specially ordered)
When available: always
Approximate cost: that of any good quality cordial
Substitute: Grand Marnier, Cointreau, or Triple Sec liqueurs; orange brandy
Importance: 4

MANDARIN ORANGE (Tangerine)

Type of food: fruit
Length: 3 in. (7.6 cm) in diameter
Shape: when whole, global with flattened top and bottom; when peeled, separates into segments
Color: orange/red skin; orange fruit segments
Consistency: fibrous but tender (like orange); juicy
Aroma: when fresh, like tangerine; when canned, more orange-like and less sharp
Taste: when fresh, like tangerine; when canned, more orange-like and less sharp
Uses: fresh peeled segments or canned segments in juice, as dessert fruit alone or mixed with other fruits and flavorings (fresh grated ginger, candied or preserved ginger, jams, jellies)
Available forms: fresh fruit; in cans; dried, sugared fruit
Storage: fresh fruit, in refrigerator — 2-3 weeks; in unopened can — indefinitely; opened can, in syrup in covered container in refrigerator — 5-7 days
When available: fresh fruit, winter months; in cans, all year
Where purchased: fruit and/or grocery shops
Approximate cost: inexpensive
Substitutes: other orange citrus fruit
Importance: 4

MANGO

Type of food: fruit
Length: 6 in. (15.2 cm)
Shape: elongated pear or avocado-shaped
Color: green with reddish-yellow streaks when ripe; cut fruit surface is orange
Surface: smooth exterior; pulpy, mildly fibrous interior
Consistency: fleshy soft, mildly fibrous
Aroma: moderately strong fruity, pleasant
Taste: pungent, fruity, unique
Uses: as dessert fruit, as nectar in fruit drink
Available forms: fresh; in syrup in cans or jars; as preserves
Storage: fresh fruit, in open air — 5-7 days; removed from can, in covered container in syrup in refrigerator — 3-5 days

When available: late winter
Where purchased: general and Chinese fruit shops; large food markets
Approximate cost: moderately expensive
Substitutes: none
Importance: 2-3

MELON SEED (*gwa tzee*)(*gwa tze*)

Type of food: dried watermelon seeds
Length: to ¼ in. (6 mm)
Shape: oval with pointed end
Color: red or black hull, white interior meat
Surface: smooth
Consistency: interior meat is chewy, crunchy
Aroma: none
Taste: nutlike, delicate, sweet
Uses: when shelled only: snack food; dessert
Available forms: by weight in sealed plastic bags
Storage: in pantry — indefinitely
When available: always
Where purchased: Chinese grocery
Approximate cost: inexpensive
Substitutes: pumpkin seeds
Importance: 3

MELON, WINTER (*dung gwa*)(*dung gwa*)

Type of food: vegetable
Length: to 21 in. (53.3 cm)
Shape: oval or round
Color: green skin; white, seedy inner meat
Surface: silvery, frosted skin; white flesh; translucent when cooked
Aroma: none
Taste: bland, delicate, subtle
Uses: candied; widely used in soups (not to be eaten raw)
Available forms: fresh by weight and by the whole melon; sugared, as a sweetmeat in plastic bags at Chinese New Year
Storage: sections, in plastic bags in refrigerator — 6 days; sugared — indefinitely
Where purchased: Chinese grocery
Approximate cost: moderately expensive
Substitutes: none
Importance: 3 (as candy)

MUSHROOMS, DRIED CHINESE (*dung gu*)(*dung gu*)
Type of food: fungus (thinner than flower mushrooms)
Length: to 2 in. (5.1 cm)
Shape: round head with stem in middle of underside
Color: black to cream
Surface: dull, ridged or ribbed, textured, shrivelled
Consistency: before soaking (inedible), brittle, dry, hard; after soaking, chewy, firm, gelatinous, meaty, moist, tender
Aroma: slight, sweet
Taste: meaty, delicate
Uses: flavoring agent, main ingredient, can be added to almost any entrée
Available forms: in plastic bags or boxes by weight
Storage: in closed jar in cool place—indefinitely
When available: always
Where purchased: Chinese grocery
Approximate cost: moderately expensive
Substitutes: flower mushroom
Importance: 4

NOODLES, CELLOPHANE (*fun see*)(*fun si*)
Type of food: noodles (made of mung bean flour); also known as bean threads, Chinese vermicelli, shining noodles, transparent noodles
Length: to 32 in. (81.3 cm) (uncooked)
Shaped: uncooked, 8-in. (20.3-cm) rectangular mats of closely wound noodles; cooked, threadlike noodles
Color: translucent
Surface: smooth, glossy, shiny
Consistency: dry (uncooked); gelatinous, moist, slippery, soft (cooked)
Aroma: none
Taste: bland, delicate; absorbs flavor of other ingredients
Uses: garnish; main ingredient
Available forms: in plastic packages
Storage: uncooked, in the pantry—indefinitely
When available: always
Where purchased: Chinese grocery

Approximate cost: inexpensive
Substitutes: egg noodles
Importance: 3

NOODLES, FRESH (*lo mein*)(*lo mein*)
Type of food: noodles (made with eggs)
Length: to 24 in. (61 cm) (cooked)
Shape: uncooked, packages of closely wound noodles; cooked, like ribbons
Color: whitish, doughy
Surface: dull
Consistency: doughy, firm
Aroma: none
Taste: bland, absorbs flavor of other ingredients
Uses: as a side dish or main ingredient in entrée
Available forms: in refrigerated packages by weight
Storage: must be refrigerated; several days or, if frozen, indefinitely
When available: always
Where purchased: Chinese grocery
Approximate cost: inexpensive
Substitutes: none
Importance: 4

PLUM WINE
Type of food: cordial, flavoring agent
Color: reddish brown
Aroma: sweet, mild, fruity
Taste: moderately strong for low-proof wine; sweet/tart, smooth, almost cordial-like
Uses: as cordial; as marinade for fruit; also as flavoring for cold and hot fruit and other sauces, toppings, punch, and frozen desserts; flavor enhancer for almost any dessert
Storage: if unopened—indefinitely; if opened and corked in cabinet—indefinitely
When available: always
Where purchased: general or Chinese liquor shops (many brands are bottled in Japan)
Approximate cost: very inexpensive
Substitutes: sherry or light fruit cordial
Importance: 4

RAMBUTAN
Type of food: fruit
Length: 1½ in. (3.8 cm)
Shape: pear-shaped; oval
Color: red outside; creamy white inside
Surface: thick, hairy outer skin
Consistency: fleshy, soft, and tender; with texture closer to the longan than to lychee
Aroma: fruity and fragrant, similar to the longan
Taste: delicate, refreshing, distinctive, somewhat more pronounced than the lychee
Uses: as dessert fruit alone or mixed with other fruits and flavorings
Available forms: in cans packed in syrup; fresh fruit not generally available outside country of origin
Storage: in unopened can—indefinitely; removed from can, in syrup in covered container in refrigerator—3–5 days
When available: always
Where purchased: in Chinese or Thai grocery shops
Substitutes: longans or, if necessary, lychees
Approximate cost: moderately expensive
Importance: 2–3

RICE, GLUTINOUS OR SWEET (*noh my*)(*noh mi*)
Type of food: grain
Length: shorter than long-grain rice
Shape: smaller and less elongated than long-grain rice
Color: creamy white
Surface: dull
Consistency: cooked, moist, pasty, slippery, tender, thick
Aroma: none
Taste: sweet, little of its own, absorbs the flavor of other ingredients
Uses: dessert, thickening agent, stuffing, main ingredient
Available forms: dry, in packages by weight; rice powder, finely ground for use in Chinese pastries
Storage: in covered jar in pantry—indefinitely
When available: always
Where purchased: Chinese grocery

Approximate cost: inexpensive
Substitutes: none
Importance: 3

SHRIMP, DRIED (*ha my*)(*sha mi*)
Type of food: shellfish
Length: ½–2 in. (13 mm to 2.5 cm)
Shape: like common variety of shrimp but very small
Color: amber
Surface: dull, shrivelled
Consistency: dry
Aroma: strong, fishy
Taste: very fishy, meaty
Uses: flavoring agent, main ingredient, stuffing
Available forms: dry, by weight in plastic bags
Storage: in covered jars—indefinitely; (if too dry, can be soaked in a little sherry or water)
When available: always
Where purchased: Chinese and Japanese groceries
Approximate cost: inexpensive
Substitutes: none
Importance: 3

SUGAR CANE DRINK
Type of food: juice, beverage
Color: translucent and pale, creamy brown
Consistency: syrupy liquid
Aroma: strong, sweet, distinctive
Taste: strong, sweet
Uses: as beverage by itself or mixed with fruit nectars or juices; flavoring agent in sauces
Available forms: in 8½-oz. (241 mL) cans
Storage: in unopened can—indefinitely; opened, in refrigerator—3–4 days
When available: in can, always
Where purchased: Chinese grocery
Approximate cost: moderately inexpensive
Substitutes: none (except other fruit juices)
Importance: 2

TOFU (DOW FOO): see BEAN CURD

SUGGESTED COMBINATIONS
FOR FRUIT CUPS, COMPOTES & SALADS

Canned fruits can generally be substituted for fresh fruits. But many canned types—peaches, apples, pears, cherries, for example—do not match the flavor, consistency, or texture of the fresh versions. Some people, however, prefer canned fruit and most of the suggested Chinese fruits are always available in cans. Some Chinese fruits, available fresh seasonally for brief periods, are usually only found in neighborhoods with large Chinese populations. Other fruits are difficult to find—fresh or canned. These include arbutus, jackfruit, palm, passion fruit, pomelo, and rambutan. Read the Guide to Ingredients for tips on availability and other characteristics.

After finding the fruits, mixing and flavoring them is another challenge. Some fruits, nuts, and seeds are better eaten alone rather than combined with other fruits. Among these are the cranberry, fig, peanut, persimmon, prune, raisin, jackfruit, palm, lotus seed, passion fruit, pumpkin, and pomegranate.

As for flavorings, ginger in all its forms—including ginger brandy—is a "universal" favorite. Fresh ginger imparts a slightly tart flavor, so you may want to add a small amount of sugar to counterbalance the tartness. Although recipes specify the amounts of ginger to use, these amounts should be adjusted to *suit your own taste*. We also suggest liqueurs—Mandarine Napoléon, Grand Marnier, and Cointreau—for flavor.

A note of caution: Be careful when preparing and serving fruits that have pits. Arbutus and lychees have one large pit; kumquats have many small pits.

When ready to mix your fruits, to please all tastes, combine one, two, or three Chinese fruits with one, two, or three from the "general" selection that follows.

Chinese

Arbutus	Longan	Mandarin orange
Date (red)	Loquat	Pomelo
Ginger	Lotus seed	Rambutan
Kumquat	Lychee	Water chestnut

General

Apple	Grapefruit	Peanut (roasted, salted, buttered, plain)
Apricot	Guava	
Banana	Honeydew melon	Pear
Blackberry	Jackfruit	Persian melon
Blueberry	Kiwi	Persimmon
Cantaloupe	Lemon	Pineapple
Casaba melon	Lime	Plum
Cherry	Lingonberry	Pomegranate
Coconut	Mango	Prune
Cranberry (whole or sauce)	Nectarine	Pumpkin
Cranshaw melon	Orange	Raisin
Currant (red and black)	Palm	Raspberry
Date	Papaya	Strawberry
Fig	Passion fruit	Watermelon
Grape (seedless and black)	Peach	

FLAVORINGS

Chinese

Almond extract
Almonds, blanched
Banana extract
Coconut
Date jam
Fruit juices, syrups, packing liquids (in the cans)
Fruits
Ginger: candied, crystallized, freshly grated, ground, preserved, preserved stem ginger

Kumquats, preserved
Liqueurs and wines: ginger brandy, Mandarine Napoléon or Grand Marnier, Midori melon liqueur, lychee wine, plum wine
Peanut butter
Plum sauce (duck sauce)
Red bean paste, sweet
Sweet preserved white cucumber
Tofu (dow foo) or bean curd
Water chestnut flour (used as thickening agent)

General

Almond
Anise
Black cherry soda (more adaptable then colas)
Cherries, maraschino
Chocolate
Chocolate coating
Cinnamon
Cointreau liqueur
Cola drinks
Cream, heavy
Fruits: canned, dried, frozen, glazed, jams and preserves, preserved
Gelatin
Grand Marnier liqueur

Grenadine syrup
Honey
Lemon: juice, grated rind
Marshmallow: bits, cream
Nondairy whipped topping
Nuts: unsalted peanuts, pecans, walnuts
Orange: juice, grated rind
Sugar: brown, white
Tapioca
Vanilla
Vinegar
Yogurt

Fruit, Jams, Jellies, Preserves

Apple
Apricot preserves
Blackberry preserves
Cherry
Currant jelly, red
Currant preserves, black
Damson plum preserves

Lingonberries in sugar
Orange marmalade
Peach preserves
Raspberry seedless preserves
Strawberry jam/preserves

SAUCES, TOPPINGS & FILLINGS

Sauces, toppings, or fillings in this cookbook add delectable touches to these baked or cooked products: angel food cake, doughnuts (plain or filled), English muffins, ladyfingers, meringues, pancakes, poundcake, puddings, shortbread dessert cakes, spongecake, sugar wafers, tapioca.

DESSERTS

Cakes

CANTONESE STEAMED CAKE (Ma-La-Gao)

馬拉糕,

2 c.	all-purpose flour	500 mL
2 t.	baking powder	10 mL
½ t.	baking soda	2 mL
4 T.	margarine	60 mL
4 T.	vegetable oil	60 mL
1½ c.	brown sugar	375 mL
4	eggs	4
2 T.	honey	30 mL
½ c.	milk	125 mL

Sift together the flour, baking powder, and soda. In a large bowl, combine margarine, oil, and brown sugar and beat well. Add eggs, one at a time, mixing well; add honey and beat well. Mix in the dry ingredients; add milk and beat thoroughly. Pour batter into a well-greased 8-in. (20-cm)-round cake pan. Steam over boiling water for 30 minutes; serve warm or cold.

Note: Cake can be reheated by steaming over boiling water for 3 to 5 minutes.

RED BEAN CAKE

紅豆糕,

1 c.	red beans	250 mL
3½ c.	water	875 mL
¼ c.	tapioca	60 mL
5 T.	sugar	75 mL
⅔ c.	cake flour	180 mL
	lard	

Wash beans in running water; drain. Soak beans in water for 3 hours. Rinse tapioca, add 2 T. (30 mL) water and let stand for an hour. Place bean mixture in saucepan, bring to a boil and cook about 1 hour; add tapioca and cook 5 minutes; add sugar and mix well. Gradually stir in flour, mixing well; pour batter into a dish greased with lard. Steam over water for 30 minutes. Cool; turn over to remove dish and cut into diamond-shaped pieces. Serve cold or hot (by resteaming).

Note: Cake can be kept in refrigerator for several days. It is particularly good when served with vanilla ice cream.

LONGAN "DRAGON EYE" BANANA CAKE

龍眼香蕉糕，

½ c.	margarine	125 mL
1½ c.	sugar	375 mL
2	eggs	2
2 c.	sifted all-purpose flour	500 mL
½ t.	baking powder	2 mL
¾ t.	baking soda	4 mL
½ t.	salt	2 mL
1 c.	bananas, mashed (2 ripe)	500 mL
¼ c.	buttermilk	60 mL
1 t.	vanilla extract	5 mL
1 c.	dried longans ("dragon eyes")	250 mL

Cream margarine and sugar; add eggs, one at a time, beating until fluffy. Sift together once the next 4 ingredients. Mix bananas and buttermilk. Grease and flour 7 × 7 × 2-in. (17 × 17 × 5-cm)-square pan. Alternately add flour and banana-buttermilk mixtures to the batter, mixing all ingredients well. Add vanilla, mixing well. Cut longans into small pieces and add to the batter. Bake at 375 °F (200 °C) for 30 to 35 minutes.

STEAMED CARROT CAKE

胡荽小糕，

1 c.	sifted all-purpose flour	250 mL
¾ t.	baking powder	4 mL
½ t.	baking soda	2 mL
1 t.	ground cardamon or cinnamon	5 mL
½ t.	salt	2 mL
½ c.	sugar	125 mL
¾ c.	peanut oil	190 mL
2	eggs	2
2 c.	carrots, shredded and chopped	500 mL
¼ c.	walnuts, raisins and dates, chopped	60 mL

Sift together once the first 6 ingredients. Add the oil, mixing thoroughly; add eggs, one at a time; mix well. Blend in carrots, nuts, raisins and dates. Pour batter into a well-greased, round cake pan and steam for 35 minutes by placing pan on a steamer over boiling water; cover the steamer.

FRESH GINGER ZUCCHINI CARROT CAKE

薑花紅綠糕，

3	eggs	3
1 c.	vegetable oil	250 mL
2½ c.	sugar	625 mL
1½ c.	zucchini (unpeeled), grated	375 mL
1½ c.	carrots, grated	375 mL
1 t.	salt	5 mL
2 t.	ground cinnamon	10 mL
1 t.	baking soda	5 mL
¼ t.	baking powder	1 mL
3 c.	all-purpose flour	750 mL

In a large mixing bowl, beat eggs until foamy; gradually beat in the oil and sugar. Add next 6 ingredients, mixing well. Gradually blend in the flour; mix well after each addition. Pour batter into greased tube or loaf pan. Bake at 350 °F (175 °C) for 1 hour. Cool in pan for 15 minutes; remove cake from pan and cool on rack. Serve sliced plain or with Ginger Sour Cream Sauce (recipe follows).

GINGER SOUR CREAM SAUCE   薑花酸奶油

1 c.	sour cream	250 mL
2 t.	fresh ginger, finely chopped	10 mL
2 t.	sugar	10 mL

Mix sour cream, ginger and sugar; spread over cake.

BANANA CAKE   香蕉糕

1 c.	margarine or butter	250 mL
3 c.	sugar	750 mL
4	eggs	4
4 c.	sifted all-purpose flour	1 L
1 t.	baking powder	5 mL
1½ t.	baking soda	7 mL
1 t.	salt	5 mL
½ c.	buttermilk	125 mL
2 c.	bananas, mashed (2–3 ripe ones)	500 mL
2 t.	vanilla extract	10 mL
2 t.	butter flavor essence (optional)	10 mL
1 c.	dates, chopped (optional)	250 mL
1 c.	raisins (optional)	250 mL

Cream butter and sugar; add eggs, one at a time, beating until fluffy. Sift together once the flour, baking powder, soda, and salt. Mix buttermilk and bananas well. Alternately add dry and buttermilk-banana mixtures, making sure all ingredients are well blended. Add butter flavor essence; fold in the dates and raisins. Pour batter into a greased and floured tube and a loaf pan. Bake at 375 °F (190 °C) or until done.

ALMOND POUND CAKE   杏仁糕

1 c.	butter or margarine (or half of each)	250 mL
2 c.	sugar	500 mL
4	eggs	4
2 t.	almond extract	10 mL
2 c.	all-purpose flour	500 mL
1 c.	almond powder (sugarless)	250 mL
¾ t.	baking powder	4 mL
½ t.	baking soda	2 mL
½ t.	salt	2 mL
1 c.	buttermilk	250 mL

Have all ingredients at room temperature. Grease 9-in. (23-cm) tube pan; line bottom with wax paper. Sift flour once; combine flour, almond powder, baking powder, soda, and salt; sift 2 more times. Cream butter and sugar. Add eggs, one at a time, mixing well. Beat in the almond extract. Add dry mixture alternately with buttermilk, beating lightly until well blended. Pour into tube pan. Bake at 350 °F (175 °C) for 1 hour or until done. Test with toothpick.

PRUNE CAKE

西枣糕

⅓ lb.	margarine	165 g
1 c.	sugar	250 mL
3	eggs	3
21 large	prunes, cooked in 1¼ c. (310 mL) water for 20 minutes, drained (save liquid), pitted and finely chopped	21 large
¾ c.	prune juice (saved after cooking prunes in water)	190 mL
2 c.	all-purpose flour	500 mL
1 t.	ground cinnamon	5 mL
1 t.	grated or ground nutmeg	5 mL
½ t.	salt	2 mL
2 t.	baking soda	10 mL

Cream the margarine and sugar until fluffy; add eggs, one at a time. Add the cooked prunes, mixing well. Mix and sift together once the flour, spices and salt. Add ½ c. (125 mL) prune juice and the flour mixture to the batter. Mix the remaining ¼ c. (60 mL) prune juice and the baking soda; add to the batter. Bake at 375 °F (190 °C) for 30 to 35 minutes. Serve with sweetened whipped cream or sour cream flavored with ½ t. (2 mL) vanilla extract and 1 T. (15 mL) sugar.

LUSCIOUS LIME SQUARES

可口酸柑糕

1 c.	margarine or butter	250 mL
½ c. plus 1T.	confectioners' sugar, more for sprinkling	140 mL
2¼ c.	all-purpose flour	560 mL
4	eggs	4
1½ c.	sugar	375 mL
½ t.	salt	2 mL
3	limes, squeezed	3
1 T.	lime rind, grated	15 mL

Cream margarine, ½ c. (125 mL) confectioners' sugar, and 2 c. (500 mL) of the flour. Pat mixture into 13 × 9-in. (33 × 23-cm) cake pan. Bake at 350 °F (175 °C) for 15 minutes. Meanwhile, beat the eggs, sugar, salt, lime juice, and rind. Sift together 1 T. (15 mL) confectioners' sugar and remaining flour. Fold into the egg mixture. Pour into the baked crust and continue baking for 30 minutes. Sift confectioners' sugar over the top. Loosen edges with a spatula; cool. Cut into squares.

LYCHEE/APRICOT NUT SQUARES

荔枝杏脯糕

3	eggs	3
¾ c.	sugar	190 mL
1 t.	vanilla extract	5 mL
¾ c.	all-purpose flour	190 mL
¾ t.	baking powder	4 mL
¾ t.	salt	4 mL

1½ c.	dried apricots, chopped	375 mL
1½ c.	dried lychees, shelled and pitted	375 mL
1½ c.	walnuts, chopped	375 mL
	confectioners' sugar	

Beat eggs until thickened; add sugar and vanilla, beating well. Sift the next 3 ingredients together and fold into the egg mixture. Add fruits and nuts, mixing well; spread batter into a well-greased 12 × 8 × 2-in. (30.5 × 20 × 5-cm) pan. Bake at 325 °F (165 °C) for 35 to 45 minutes or until golden brown. When cold, cut into squares and sprinkle with confectioners' sugar. Squares can be frozen.

DATE NUT SQUARES

蜜枣核桃糕

3	eggs	3
¾ c.	sugar	190 mL
1 t.	vanilla extract	5 mL
¾ c.	all-purpose flour	190 mL
¾ t.	baking powder	4 mL
¾ t.	salt	4 mL
1½ c.	dates or dried apricots, chopped	375 mL
1½ c.	raisins	375 mL
1½ c.	walnuts, chopped	375 mL
	confectioners' sugar	

Beat eggs until thickened; add sugar and vanilla, beating well. Sift together the flour, baking powder, and salt; fold flour mixture into the egg mixture. Add remaining ingredients, mixing well. Spread batter in well-greased 12 × 8 × 2-in. (30.5 × 20 × 5-cm) pan. Bake at 325 °F (165 °C) for 35 to 45 minutes or until golden brown; cool. Cut into squares and garnish with confectioners' sugar.

YUMMY YAM CAKE

香甜红薯糕

2 c.	all-purpose flour	500 mL
2 t.	baking powder	10 mL
½ t.	baking soda	2 mL
¼ t.	salt	1 mL
½ t.	ground cardamon	2 mL
1 t.	ground nutmeg	5 mL
1 t.	ground cinnamon	5 mL
½ t.	ground cloves	2 mL
3	eggs	3
1 c.	peanut oil	250 mL
1½ c.	sugar	375 mL
2 c. (about 1 lb.)	uncooked yam, grated	500 mL (about 450 g)
½ c.	chopped nuts	125 mL
⅓ c.	hot water	90 mL

Sift together once the first 8 ingredients. Separate the egg yolks from the whites; beat the whites until firm. In a large mixing bowl, combine oil and sugar, beating well. Add yolks and beat thoroughly. Mix in the yam and nuts. Alternately blend dry mixture and the hot water with the batter; fold in the beaten egg whites. Pour batter into well-greased cake pan, lined with wax paper. Bake at 350 °F (175 °C) for about 1 hour or until done. Before removing cake from pan, cool on rack for 15 minutes.

NOODLE CAKE (Sha-Ke-Ma)

西騎馬

2 c.	cake flour	500 mL
½ t.	ammonium bicarbonate	2 mL
1½ t.	baking powder	7 mL
3	eggs	3
4 c.	peanut oil for deep-frying	1 L
1¼ c.	sugar	310 mL
⅔ c.	maltose	180 mL
1 c.	water	250 mL
1 t.	white vinegar	5 mL
1 T.	sesame seeds	15 mL
½ c.	walnuts, chopped	125 mL

Combine the first 3 ingredients and sift into a bowl. Make a well in the middle of the flour mixture and break the eggs into the well. Mix by hand, kneading until the dough is smooth and elastic. On a floured board, roll dough into ⅛-in. (3-mm)-thick sheet; cut into 2-in. (5.1-cm)-long strips; dust strips lightly with flour. To fry the strips, heat oil; deep-fry the strips over medium heat until golden; remove and drain until dry. Spread fried strips on a greased square pan.

To make the syrup, mix the sugar, maltose, water, and vinegar in a saucepan; bring to a boil, then simmer over low heat. Stir until mixture thickens and forms a thread when dripped from spoon. Pour syrup immediately over the strips and mix well. Toast the sesame seeds by heating in an ungreased pan over low heat until light brown. Mix sesame seeds with the walnuts; spread mixture over the strips; and press down with your hand to make a 1½-in. (3.8-cm)-high cake. Cut the cake into 1½ × 2½-in. (3.8 × 6.4-cm) pieces, using a sharp knife. Serve cold or freeze until ready to serve. Thaw before serving.

GINGER JAM JELLY ROLL

3	eggs	3
1 c.	sugar	250 mL
⅓ c.	water	90 mL
1 t.	vanilla extract	5 mL
1 c.	cake flour	250 mL
¼ t.	salt	1 mL
	confectioners' sugar	
⅔ c.	ginger preserves (marmalade)	180 mL
½ c.	pecans or walnuts, finely chopped	125 mL

Line a 15½ × 10½ × 1-in. (39 × 25 × 3-cm) jelly roll pan with aluminum foil or wax paper; grease the paper. In a mixing bowl, beat eggs about 5 minutes or until very thick and lemon-colored. Gradually beat in the sugar. Blend in the water and vanilla on low speed; gradually add flour and salt; beat until batter is smooth. Pour into the pan and spread batter to the corners. Bake at 375 °F (190 °C) for 12 to 15 minutes or until toothpick inserted into middle comes out clean. Loosen cake from edges; turn onto towel sprinkled with the confectioners' sugar; remove foil from bottom of cake. While hot, roll cake and towel from narrow end; place on wire rack to cool. Unroll cake and remove towel. Beat preserves with fork to soften; mix with the nuts, then spread the mixture over the cake. Roll cake and sprinkle outside with confectioners' sugar.

Clockwise from top: sweet melon, dried pineapple, orange peel, sweet coconut, sweet papaya, dried mango.

Clockwise from top: chestnut, water chestnut, dried longan, dried lychee, dried lotus seed.

Arbutus.

Loquat.

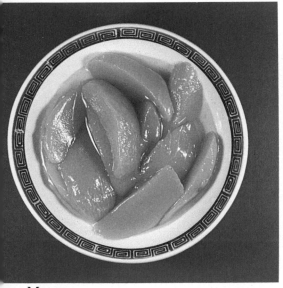

Mango.

Palm seed.

Longan.

Preserved kumquat.

Mandarin orange.

Lychee.

Clockwise from top: candied kumquat, crystallized ginger slices, preserved sweetened stem ginger, preserved red dates, preserved lemon slices.

Clockwise from top: assorted preserved fruits, walnut date candy, peanut sesame candy, sesame cake, peanut cake.

DOUGHNUT SLICES WITH CHINESE FLAVORS

6	plain or sugared doughnuts	6
	sweet bean paste or date jam or ginger preserves or preserved kumquats	

Slice doughnuts into ½-in. (1.3-cm) slices. Spread desired filling ingredient between the slices to make a small sandwich; or spread on top of cut surface as a topping.

Note: Doughnut slices or whole doughnuts can be served with various sauces in this cookbook.

GOLDEN NUT CAKE

3	eggs	3
1½ c.	sugar	375 mL
1½ t.	vanilla extract	7 ml
1½ c.	all-purpose flour	375 mL
1½ t.	baking powder	7 mL
1 t.	salt	5 mL
¾ c.	milk	190 mL
1 T.	peanut oil	15 mL
½ c.	brown sugar	125 mL
6 T.	butter, melted	90 mL
3 T.	evaporated milk or cream	45 mL
1 c.	walnuts, chopped	250 ml
1–1½ c.	shredded coconut	250–375 mL

Combine the first 6 ingredients and mix well. In a saucepan, combine milk and oil; bring to a boil. Add the milk mixture to the egg mixture and beat until batter is smooth. Pour into greased 12 × 8 × 2-in. (30.5 × 20 × 5-cm) pan. Bake at 350 °F (175 °C) until cake is golden brown, 40 to 45 minutes. While cake is baking, mix remaining ingredients to make a topping. When cake is done and still hot, spread the mixture on top. Place cake 2 in. (5.1 cm) below a preheated broiler; brown for 2-3 minutes until golden brown, but not burnt; serve hot or cold.

GLUTINOUS (SWEET) RICE CAKE

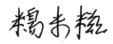

1 lb.	sweet rice flour (mo chiko)	450 g
3 c.	water	750 mL
¾–1 c.	sugar, to taste	190–250 mL
1 lb.	black bean paste (dow sa)	450 g
	cornstarch	

Mix the rice flour, water, and sugar, beating until well mixed and smooth. Place mixture in 17 × 11 × 2-in. (43.2 × 27.9 × 5-cm)-square pan. Steam over boiling water about 30 minutes, until inserted chopstick will come out clean. Pour off any excess of the cooking mixture. While mixture is still warm, dust hands with cornstarch and take about 1 T. (15 mL) of the mixture, shaping it into a circle. Place 1 T. (15 mL) bean paste in middle of each circle; pinch and seal edge together to enfold the filling. Roll into a ball; then flatten ball slightly. (If ball is sticky, dust hands with more cornstarch.) Cakes can be stored in a sealed bag for a few days or stored in freezer for weeks.

WALNUT TORTE

核桃鬆糕,

4	eggs	4
1 c.	sugar	250 mL
1 c.	bread crumbs	250 mL
1 t.	baking powder	5 mL
1 c.	walnuts, finely chopped	250 mL
1 recipe	Walnut Frosting (recipe follows)	1 recipe

Separate the eggs; beat whites until they stand in soft peaks. Gradually add ½ c. (125 mL) of the sugar; beat until stiff. In another bowl, beat the yolks; add remaining ½ c. (125 mL) sugar; beating until very thick and light in color. Blend in the bread crumbs and baking powder, mixing well; add the nuts. With a spoon, fold the whites into the yolk mixture. Grease 2 8-in. (20-cm)-round layer pans; line with wax paper. Pour batter into pans. Bake at 375 °F (190 °C) for 20 minutes or until done; cool. Top with Walnut Frosting.

WALNUT FROSTING

薑花酸奶油

2 c.	heavy cream	500 mL
½ t.	vanilla extract	2 mL
2 t.	sugar	10 mL
¼ c.	walnuts, finely chopped	60 mL

Whip the cream; gradually add the vanilla and sugar. Fold in the walnuts. Refrigerate until ready to spread on the torte.

MERINGUE SHELLS

蛋白酥皮

6	egg whites	6
¼ t.	salt	1 mL
¾ t.	cream of tartar	4 mL
1½ c.	sugar	375 mL

Beat egg whites with salt and cream of tartar until frothy. Gradually add the sugar, continuing to beat until peaks are stiff and sugar dissolves. With a spoon, shape into 12 shell cups on a baking sheet lined with unglazed paper. Bake shells at 250 °F (120 °C) for 1 hour. Transfer shells from paper to wire racks to cool.

Cookies, Bars & Squares

SESAME COOKIES

2 c.	all-purpose flour	500 mL
2 t.	baking powder	10 mL
½ c.	sugar	125 mL
⅛ t.	salt	.5 mL
½ c.	margarine or lard	125 mL
¼ c.	cold water	60 mL
1 t.	vanilla extract	5 mL
1	egg white, lightly beaten	1
	sesame seeds	

Sift together the first 4 ingredients into a bowl. Blend in the margarine; add water and vanilla, mixing well. Place dough on wax paper that has been dusted with flour. Shape into 2 rolls, about 1½ in. (3.8 cm) in diameter. Leave roll on wax paper and chill in refrigerator for 2 hours. Slice dough into ¼-in. (6-mm) pieces. Coat each piece with egg white; then dip the cut sides into sesame seeds. Place cookies on an ungreased cookie sheet. Bake at 350 °F (175 °C) for 20 to 25 minutes or until golden brown.

ANISE COOKIES

4	eggs	4
2 c.	sugar	500 mL
4 c.	sifted all-purpose flour	1 L
1 t.	baking soda	5 mL
2 t.	anise extract	10 mL

Beat eggs with sugar until fluffy, light. Gradually stir in the flour, baking soda, and extract; blend well to form dough; refrigerate for 1 hour. Divide into 3 parts. Roll out each part, using a rolling pin on a floured pastry cloth or board until ¼-in. (6-mm) thick, adding flour to board when needed. Cut individual cookies with cookie cutter. Place 1 in. (2.5 cm) apart on buttered cookie sheets; brush off excess flour. Let stand overnight uncovered. Bake at 300 °F (150 °C) for 15 minutes or until dry and firm. Remove to wire racks to cool. Store in tightly covered container for about a week before eating.

PINE-NUTS ALMOND COOKIES

松子杏仁餅

1 c.	margarine	250 mL
1 c.	sugar	250 mL
2	egg yolks	2
1 t.	vanilla extract	5 mL
1½ t.	almond extract	7 mL
1½ c.	all-purpose flour	375 mL
½ c.	sugarless almond powder	125 mL
1 t.	baking powder	5 mL
1	egg white, lightly beaten	1
½ c.	pine nuts	125 mL

Cream margarine and sugar. Add yolks and flavorings; mix thoroughly. Sift together the flour, almond powder, and baking powder and add gradually to the batter, mixing until well blended. Refrigerate for 45 minutes.

Roll about 1 T. (15 mL) of the dough into a ball; flatten slightly into a round cookie; dip one side into the egg white, then press on enough pine nuts to cover. With seeded side up, place cookies on ungreased cookie sheet about 2-in. (5-cm) apart. Bake at 325 °F (165 °C) until golden brown, about 18 to 25 minutes. Before removing from cookie sheet, cool 5 minutes. Makes approximately 30 cookies.

COCONUT-FRUIT-NUT BARS

椰絲果仁餅

Crust

½ c.	butter and margarine	125 mL
1 c.	brown sugar	250 mL
2 c.	sifted all-purpose flour	500 mL

Cream butter, margarine, and brown sugar; add the flour, mixing until crumbly. Spread evenly in greased 7 × 11 × 2-in. (17 × 27.9 × 5-cm) pan. Bake at 350 °F (175 °C) for about 15 minutes; cool.

Filling

4	eggs	4
2 c.	brown sugar	500 mL
¼ c.	all-purpose flour	60 mL
½ t.	baking soda	2 mL
½ t.	salt	2 mL
1	lemon	1
2 c.	shredded coconut	500 mL
1½ c.	walnuts	375 mL
1½ c.	raisins	375 mL

To make the filling, beat eggs until foamy; add the sugar and beat well. Mix and sift together the flour, baking soda, and salt. Squeeze the lemon and add with the flour mixture to the eggs, mixing well. Add coconut, nuts, and raisins; mix well. Pour filling into the baked crust. Bake for 30 minutes at 350 °F (175 °C). Cool completely on rack; then cut into squares.

ALMOND DREAM BARS

杏仁椰絲糕

½ c.	margarine or butter	125 mL
¼ c.	confectioners' sugar	60 mL
1 c.	sifted all-purpose flour	250 mL
2	eggs	2
1 c.	light brown sugar	250 mL
3 T.	all-purpose flour	45 mL
1 t.	baking powder	5 mL
dash	salt	dash
½ t.	almond extract	2 mL
1 c.	almonds, slivered	250 mL
1 c.	flaked or shredded coconut	250 mL

Cream margarine and sugar until smooth. With hand, work in 1 c. (250 mL) flour until mixture is blended and smooth. Pat into bottom of 13 × 9 × 2-in. (33 × 22.9 × 5-cm) pan. Bake at 350 °F (175 °C) for about 10 to 12 minutes until golden. Cool on wire rack. Beat eggs until light; gradually beat in the light brown sugar. Add 3 T. (45 mL) flour, baking powder, salt, and almond extract, mixing well. Stir in the almonds and coconut. Spread batter evenly over baked and cooled base. Bake again until golden and firm to the touch, about 25 minutes. Cut into bars when slightly cooled.

PLAIN ALMOND COOKIES

杏仁餅

½ c.	butter	125 mL
½ c.	margarine	125 mL
1 c.	sugar	250 mL
2	egg yolks	2
1½ t.	almond extract	7 mL
1 t.	vanilla extract	5 mL
2 c.	all-purpose flour	500 mL
1 t.	baking powder	5 mL
1	egg white, lightly beaten	1

Cream butter, margarine and sugar; add yolks and flavorings, mixing well. Sift together the flour and baking powder. Add flour mixture gradually to the creamed mixture, beating until well blended. Refrigerate dough for 45 minutes.

Roll about 1 T. (15 mL) of the dough into a ball; continue making balls. Flatten balls slightly into round cookies. Dip into the egg white. Place cookies on ungreased cookie sheet for 2 in. (5 cm) apart. Bake at 325 °F (165 °C) until golden brown, for 18 to 25 minutes. Before removing from cookie sheet, cool 5 minutes. Makes approximately 30 cookies.

Fritters & Pancakes

BANANA FRITTERS WITH ORIENTAL LIQUEUR

甜酒香蕉酥

4 firm	bananas without brown spots	4 firm
3 T.	confectioners' sugar	45 mL
2 T.	lemon juice	30 mL
1½ T.	plum wine or Mandarine Napoléon liqueur	22.5 mL
1⅓ c.	sifted all-purpose flour	340 mL
2 T.	sugar	30 mL
1 t.	baking powder	5 mL
½ t.	salt	2 mL
2	egg yolks	2
1 T.	margarine or butter	15 mL
⅔ c.	milk	180 mL
1 t.	vanilla extract	5 mL
2	egg whites	2
¼ c.	all-purpose flour	60 mL
	peanut oil for deep frying	
¼ c.	sugar	60 mL

Peel bananas and cut them crosswise into 1½-in. (3.8-cm) slices. In a bowl, gently toss bananas with confectioners' sugar, lemon juice, and liqueur. Cover bowl and marinate 55 minutes, gently stirring occasionally. Mix together the flour, sugar, baking powder, and salt. In another bowl, beat egg yolks until thick. Melt the margarine or butter and add to the yolks with the milk and vanilla, beating constantly. Drain liquid from the banana mixture and add to yolks. Make a well in the middle of the flour mixture; pour the yolk mixture in and blend until batter is smooth. Beat egg whites until rounded peaks are formed; gently fold into the batter. Coat pieces of marinated banana by rolling in the flour. Using a large fork, dip pieces of banana into the batter and coat evenly; drain excess batter fom banana. Heat the oil to 365 °F (184 °C) and deep-fry bananas for 2 to 3 minutes or until golden brown. Drain over oil, then place on paper towel. Sprinkle with sugar and serve hot.

Note: For tasty variations: Substitute 3 apples, peeled, cored, and cut into ¼-in. (6-mm)-thick slices; or 7 peaches, pitted, and cut into 8 segments; or drained, canned lychees or longans for the bananas.

LYCHEE FRITTERS

荔枝油燆餅

20-oz. can	lychees	565-g can
1 c.	all-purpose flour	250 mL
1 t.	baking powder	5mL
1 t.	salt	5 mL
2	eggs	2
½ c.	milk	125 mL
1 t.	vegetable oil	5 mL
3 c.	peanut oil	750 mL
	ground cinnamon	

Drain lychees and reserve the juice; dry lychees on paper towel. In a bowl, mix the next 6 ingredients; beat until smooth. Using chopsticks or fork, dip lychees in the flour mixture individually. Heat oil to 325 °F (165 °C) in a deep fryer. Fry coated lychees in hot oil about 3 minutes *or* until browned. Drain on paper towel. Sprinkle sparingly with cinnamon or confectioners' sugar and serve.

Note: If you prefer, substitute canned loquats or longans, or sliced banana segments for the lychees.

PEANUT FRITTERS

花生油燆餅

1 c.	rice flour	250 mL
1 t.	baking powder	5 mL
2 t.	ground coriander	10 mL
1 t.	salt	5 mL
¼ t.	pepper	1 mL
1 t.	onion, chopped	5 mL
1–2 cloves	garlic, chopped	1–2 cloves
¾ c.	coconut milk	190 mL
1	egg, beaten	1
¼ lb.	skinless raw peanuts	120 g
2 c.	peanut oil	500 mL

Sift together the first 5 ingredients. Add remaining ingredients except the oil; mix well. In a skillet, heat oil to the smoking point. Ladle the peanut mixture onto the skillet; fry until golden brown, turning several times with chopsticks. Drain on paper towel before serving.

BANANA PANCAKES

香蕉鍋餅

1 c.	all-purpose flour	250 mL
1 t.	baking powder	5 mL
¼ t.	salt	1 mL
2 T.	sugar	30 mL
2	eggs	2
½ c.	milk	125 mL
1 c.	bananas mashed	250 mL
	vegetable oil	

Sift together the first 4 ingredients; beat eggs; add milk, mixing thoroughly. Combine flour mixture with the egg mixture; add bananas and mix well. Grease skillet with 1 t. (5 mL) oil and heat pan over medium heat. Add about ¼ to ½ c. (60 to 125 mL) of the batter; when bubbles show, turn over and fry until golden brown.

FRIED BEAN PASTE PANCAKE

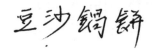

2	eggs	2
⅔ c.	all-purpose flour	180 mL
2 T.	cornstarch	30 mL
½ t.	baking powder	2 mL
⅔ c.	water	180 mL
4 oz.	bean paste	125 mL
	vegetable oil for deep frying	

Beat eggs, then add flour, cornstarch, and baking powder; mix well. Gradually add the water, beating steadily. Heat an 8-in. (20-cm) skillet; grease pan with 1 T. (15 mL) oil. Add one-fourth the batter, swirling it to cover bottom of pan and make a thin pancake. Cook over low heat for a few seconds; remove to a dish, uncooked side up. Place 1 oz. (30 g) bean paste in middle of pancake; spread to make a 2 × 6-in. (5.1 × 15.2-cm) rectangle; fold pancake over to form an envelope and seal with a little batter. Heat 2 c. (500 mL) oil until hot; deep-fry pancakes until golden brown and crispy, about 1 to 2 minutes. Remove to a dish, cut into pieces and serve hot.

Pastries

ALMOND CUSTARD TARTS

杏仁蛋撻餅

2	eggs	2
1 c.	milk	250 mL
2½ T.	sugar	37.5 mL
1 t.	almond extract	5 mL
6 small	prebaked tart shells	6 small

Beat eggs well. Add milk, sugar, and almond extract, mixing thoroughly. Pour into tart shells. Bake at 375 °F (190 °C) for 30 minutes or until toothpick inserted in middle of custard comes out clean. Remove from oven. Serve at room temperature.

WHITE PEACH TART

白桃烘餅

⅓ c.	sugar	90 mL
4 T.	sweet butter	60 mL
4 oz.	marzipan almond paste	120 g
2	eggs	2
2 t.	peach liqueur	10 mL
	Sweet Piecrust, partially baked	
½ c.	peach jam	125 mL
1 T.	water	15 mL
1 T.	peach liqueur	15 mL
8½-oz. can	Chinese white or yellow cling peaches, drained and cut into slices	241-g can

Cream sugar, butter, and almond paste; process until smooth and well blended. Add eggs, 1 at a time; beat until smooth. Add the liqueur and mix. Pour mixture into partially baked piecrust. Bake at 350 °F (175 °C) for approximately 30 minutes or until middle is puffed and evenly browned. Cool on rack, then remove from pan. Mix jam, water, and liqueur in a saucepan and heat until jam melts, stirring occasionally; remove from heat and cool. Arrange sliced peaches over baked tart. Glaze with the jam mixture.

LYCHEE/CHERRY PIE

¼ t.	fresh ginger	1 mL
1½ T.	ginger preserves	22.5 mL
7	lychees, coarsely chopped	7
½ t.	plum wine	2 mL
21-oz. can	cherry pie filling	595-g can
	Sweet Piecrust	

Mix the ginger, preserves, lychees, and wine with one-third the cherry filling. Pour into baked piecrust and follow directions for baking White Peach Tart.

Note: You may substitute the following flavorful combinations: blueberry or apple pie filling for the cherry filling, using only 1 T. (15 mL) ginger preserves; flavor with ¼ t. (1 mL) Mandarine Napoléon or Grand Marnier liqueur for the plum wine. For more Chinese flavor, use longans, loquats, or rambutans for the suggested fruit.

SWEET PIECRUST

2 c.	all-purpose flour	500 mL
½ c.	sugar	125 mL
1 c.	butter, at room temperature	250 mL
2 large	egg yolks	2 large
½ t.	vanilla extract	2 mL

Combine flour and sugar in a bowl. Slice butter; using a pastry blender, blend into flour and sugar mixture until it resembles dry meal. Add the yolks and vanilla, mixing to make a soft dough. Spread the dough about ⅛ in. (3 mm) thick into a 9-in. (23-cm) tart pan with a removable bottom. Press dough into corners, making sure it is evenly distributed; trim edges off top. Bake at 350 °F (175 °C) for 8 to 10 minutes. Cool slightly, then fill with desired filling.

Confections

ELEVEN PRECIOUS INGREDIENTS STUFFED LYCHEES 什锦荔枝

20-oz. can	*lychees*	565-g can
	chocolate candy-bar shavings;	
	lingonberries drained;	
	orange marmalade; date	
	jam; ginger marmalade;	
	preserved kumquats, pitted,	
	finely chopped; pineapple	
	chunks, coarsely chopped;	
	mandarin orange segment	
	or fresh orange segment;	
	peach jam or apricot	
	preserves; currant jelly;	
	strawberry jam or seedless	
	raspberry jam	

Drain lychees and save the juice. Dry lychees on paper towel, rolling about carefully for 15 seconds. Stuff lychees with an appropriate amount of above selection of ingredients, using 1 ingredient for each.

Note: For variations of this recipe, you may substitute longans or rambutans for the lychees. To add more flavor, before stuffing each lychee, longan, or rambutan, sprinkle 2 drops plum wine, Mandarine Napoléon or Grand Marnier liqueur into each fruit.

APRICOT-KUMQUAT BALLS 杏脯柑橘球

4	*glazed apricots*	4
5–6	*preserved kumquats, seeded*	5–6
½ c.	*sugar, spread evenly on a plate*	125 mL

Cut apricots and kumquats into ½-in. (1.3-cm) strips; chop coarsely. Mix and shape the fruits into balls. Roll balls in the sugar. Store in covered containers.

APRICOTS STUFFED WITH GINGER

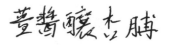

1 lb.	dried apricots	450 g
	ginger preserves	
	sugar	

Steam apricots 15 minutes in a covered colander; cool. Place ½ t. (2 mL) preserves on each apricot and fold to cover fillings. Roll (stuffed apricots) in sugar.

Note: If apricots are small, place preserves on top of a half, cover with another half, press together and roll in sugar.

FROSTED LYCHEES

15	canned lychees, chilled	15
1	egg white, at room temperature	1
½ c.	sugar	125 mL

Thoroughly drain lychees and save the liquid. Beat egg white until stiff. Coat the chilled lychees with beaten egg white. Sprinkle sugar thinly on a dessert plate. Using chopsticks or fork, roll lychees in the sugar. Place lychees on wire rack or large plate and allow to dry for 5 minutes. Reroll lychees in sugar. Serve at once.

Note: To make Frosted Kumquats, substitute 14 preserved kumquats for the lychees.

ORANGE SESAME STRIPS

2 T.	sugar	30 mL
½ c.	orange juice	125 mL
¼ oz.	package unflavored gelatin	8 g
6 drops	lemon extract	6 drops
	sesame seeds, toasted (optional)	

Combine sugar and orange juice in a saucepan. Heat, stirring until sugar melts; simmer 1 minute. Remove from heat, stir in the gelatin until mixture is smooth; add lemon extract. Pour into plastic-lined 7-in. (17-cm)-square pan. Sprinkle with sesame seeds, if using. Chill in refrigerator. Cut into strips before serving.

YAM OR SWEET POTATO TOFFEE

1 lb.	yams or sweet potatoes	450 g
	peanut oil for cooking	
6 T.	brown sugar	90 mL
2 T.	water	30 mL
1 T.	malted sugar or honey	15 mL
	sesame seeds	
	ice water	

Peel and wash yams, cut into ¾-in. (1.9-cm) pieces, and dry with paper towel. Heat 2 c. (500 mL) of the oil in a deep fryer; add yam pieces, a few at a time; deep-fry until golden brown (when cooked, they will float to top). Drain on paper towel. In a saucepan, heat 1 T. (15 mL) of the oil. Add brown sugar, water, and malted sugar; continue stirring over low heat until syrup forms a thread when poured from spoon, or when a drop of syrup in bowl of cold water forms a ball. Add fried yam to syrup, stirring well; then place on a greased platter. Sprinkle with sesame seeds, dip in ice water, and serve.

NATURAL DRIED FRUITS STUFFED WITH ORIENTAL DELIGHTS

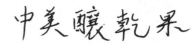

Many fruits make delicious combinations with Chinese preserved foods. The following fruits can be combined with any stuffing indicated below with an asterisk (*). Those that cannot be combined are marked with a dagger (†).

	preserved kumquat	preserved ginger in syrup	ginger preserves	crystallized ginger	date jam	sweet red bean paste	preserved white cucumber
Pitted prunes	*	*	*	*	*	*	*
Papaya	*	*	*	*	*	*	†
Figs	*	*	†	*	*	†	†
Pineapple	*	*	†	*	*	*	†
Apricots	*	*	*	*	*	*	*
Crystallized ginger	*	†	†	†	*	*	†
Dates	*	*	†	*	*	†	*
Peaches	*	*	*	*	*	*	†
Pears	*	*	*	*	*	*	†
Apple	*	*	*	*	*	*	*

Cut chosen stuffing into symmetrical bite-sized pieces. Spoon oriental stuffing onto half of the fruit. Cover with other half and lightly press halves together. Roll edges of sandwich in granulated sugar and spread out on large dish. Set aside, covered until ready to serve.

HONEY-DIPPED GLAZED FRUITS STUFFED WITH ORIENTAL DELIGHTS

	preserved kumquat, chopped	preserved ginger in syrup, sliced	ginger preserves	crystallized ginger	date jam	sweet red bean paste	preserved white cucumber, coarsely chopped
Apricots	*	*	*	*	*	*	*
Peaches	*	*	*	*	*	*	†
Apples	*	*	*	†	*	*	*
Quince	*	*	*	†	*	*	†
Pears	*	*	*	*	*	*	†
Orange glaze	*	*	*	*	*	*	*
Papaya	*	*	*	*	*	*	†
Pineapple	*	*	*	*	*	*	*

Prepare fruit and stuff the same as Natural Dried Fruits Stuffed with Oriental Delights. Combinations marked with an asterisk (*) can be combined; those with a dagger (†) *cannot* be combined.

ASSORTED STUFFED DRIED FRUITS

Substitute dried peaches, prunes, or pears for dried apricots. Steam the dried fruits 15 minutes in a covered colander; cool. Substitute ½ t. (2 mL) of one of the following for the ginger preserves: preserved kumquats, coarsely chopped; sliced ginger in syrup; date jam; sweet red bean paste.

Note: ½ t. (2 mL) Mandarine Napoléon or Grand Marnier liqueur can be mixed with the filling.

COCONUT KISSES

椰絲糖

3	egg whites	3
½ c.	sugar	125 mL
2 c.	shredded coconut	500 mL
1 t.	vanilla extract	5 mL
	butter	
	all-purpose flour	

Beat egg whites 10 minutes, gradually adding the sugar. Add the coconut and vanilla. Butter baking pans and sprinkle lightly with flour. Drop mixture from end of spoon into pans. Bake kisses at 325 °F (165 °C) until firm.

ORIENTAL ALMOND GEL CANDY

杏仁膠糖

2 env.	unflavored gelatin	2 env.
½ c.	cold water	125 mL
¾ c.	water	190 mL
2 c.	sugar	500 mL
pinch	salt	pinch
1 t.	almond extract	5 mL
	confectioners' sugar	

Soften gelatin in cold water. Combine next 4 ingredients in a saucepan and slowly bring to a boil. Add gelatin mixture, stirring until dissolved. Boil gently 15 minutes; remove from heat. Add almond extract. Pour into 8-in. (23-cm) pan which has been rinsed in cold water. Refrigerate until firm, about 12 hours. With wet knife, loosen gel from edges of pan. Sift confectioners' sugar on top of gel and cut into squares. Serve sprinkled with additional sugar.

CHOCOLATE-DIPPED LYCHEES

荔枝沾巧克力

| 12 | lychees |
| | Smucker's Magic Shell chocolate topping, heated |

Thoroughly dry the lychees on a paper towel; arrange on a plate. Pour the topping over the lychees, coating thoroughly; refrigerate. (The chocolate hardens when chilled.) Arrange on a clean plate. Serve chilled.

Note: For variations on Chocolate-Dipped Lychees, substitute longans, loquats, rambutans, preserved stem ginger cut into ¼-in. (6-mm) pieces, or preserved kumquats for the lychees.

CHOCOLATE-DIPPED FORTUNE COOKIES

簽語餅沾巧克力

| 12 | fortune cookies |
| | Smucker's Magic Shell chocolate topping, heated |

Arrange fortune cookies on a flat plate. Pour the topping over the rounded ends. Refrigerate and serve chilled on a clean plate.

Note: You may substitute almond cookies or other Chinese cookies, such as *fung won* rolls for the fortune cookies. Coat one side of the cookies.

Nuts & Seeds

GLAZED ALMONDS

½ c.   *honey*   125 mL
         margarine
1 c.   *shelled almonds* 250 mL

蜜饯杏仁

Boil honey in a small saucepan over low heat for about 15 minutes; allow froth to settle. (If honey hardens before being used up, reheat until it liquefies.) Rub dinner plate lightly with margarine. Drop almonds into hot honey, stirring with a slotted spoon until almonds are well coated. Scoop almonds onto plate and separate each with clean knife. Allow almonds to cool and harden. Scrape almonds off plate and separate before serving.

ROASTED CASHEWS

1 lb.   *raw cashew nuts* 450 g
1¼ t.   *salt, to taste*   6 mL

烤腰果

Rinse nuts in cold water; drain in colander. Add salt and toss well. Line a cookie sheet with aluminum foil. Spread nuts evenly over foil. Bake at 275 °F (135 °C) for 30 minutes. Remove from oven and turn nuts over; bake 10 minutes longer. Turn again and bake 12 more minutes. Cool completely. Store in airtight container.

HOLIDAY LOTUS SEEDS WITH FRUIT FLAVOR

果香蓮子

40   *sugared lotus seeds*   40
       lychee juice to cover seeds
1 t.   *black currant preserves or red currant preserves* 5 mL
1 t.   *seedless red raspberry preserves*   5 mL
¼ t. *lemon juice*   1 mL

Mix all ingredients; marinate for 2 hours. Serve at room temperature or chilled.

ROASTED PEANUTS

烤花生

1 lb.   *skinless raw peanuts* 450 g
1 t.   *salt, to taste*   5 mL

Wash peanuts in cold water; drain immediately. Add salt and mix well in a colander. Spread peanuts on a cookie sheet. Bake at 275 °F (135 °C) for 30 minutes. Stir and bake for 10 more minutes. Stir once more and bake 10 more minutes; cool. Store in an airtight container in a cool place.

FIVE SPICES SWEET-SALTY PEANUTS

五香花生

1	egg white	1
1 T.	water	15 mL
1½ t.	five spices powder (wu shiang fun)	7 mL
½ t.	salt, to taste	2 mL
2 T.	sugar, to taste	30 mL
1 lb.	unsalted roasted peanuts	450 g

In a small bowl, beat egg white and water until frothy; add the seasonings, mixing well; stir in the peanuts and coat thoroughly. Spread peanuts on ungreased or foil-lined cookie sheet. Bake at 275 °F (135 °C), stirring every 15 minutes, until light brown and crisp, about 45 to 50 minutes; cool. Store in tightly sealed jar in the refrigerator.

FIVE SPICES UNSALTED PEANUTS

五香淡花生

1 lb.	roasted peanuts	450 g
1	egg white	1
1 T.	water	15 mL
1–1½ t.	five spices powder	5–7 mL

Place peanuts in a large bowl. Beat egg white and water in a small bowl until frothy; add the spice, mixing well. Pour mixture over the peanuts and coat thoroughly. Spread on a cookie sheet. Bake at 275 °F (135 °C), stirring every 15 minutes, until light brown and crisp, about 45 to 55 minutes; cool. Store in airtight container in a cool place.

CANDIED WALNUTS

合桃糖

¾ c.	water	190 mL
1 c.	sugar	250 mL
⅛ t.	cream of tartar	.5 mL
½ lb.	shelled walnuts	225 g

Mix water, sugar, and cream of tartar in a saucepan. Stir over low heat until sugar dissolves. Bring to a boil and cook until dripping syrup forms threads in cold water; remove from heat. Using chopsticks, dip each walnut in syrup to cover. Place each walnut on lightly greased plate to cool.

WALNUT STRIPS

合桃条.

½ c.	all-purpose flour	125 mL
⅛ t.	salt	.5 mL
2	eggs	2
⅔ c.	brown sugar	180 mL
1 c.	walnuts, chopped	250 mL
½ c.	butter	125 mL
⅓ c.	confectioners' sugar	90 mL
1 t.	instant coffee	5 mL
½ c.	walnuts, chopped for garnish	125 mL

Sift together the flour and salt. Beat eggs until lemon-colored; gradually mix in the brown sugar, beating well. Add the flour mixture and the walnuts, stirring well. Grease 7-in. (17-cm) square pan and dust with flour. Pour batter into pan. Bake at 350 °F (175 °C) for 30 minutes; cool on rack for 10 minutes. Remove cake to a plate. While cake is cooling, mix butter and confectioners' sugar until well blended; add coffee and mix well. Spread mixture on top of cake; garnish with walnuts and cut into strips.

Beverages

WATER CHESTNUT/PEANUT BUTTER DRINK 馬蹄花生醬露

2 T.	water chestnut starch or cornstarch	30 mL
2 T.	water	30 mL
2 T.	peanut butter	30 mL
1¾ c.	water	440 mL
1–1½ T.	sugar	15–22.5 mL

Mix starch and 2 T (30 mL) water in a 1-qt. (1-L) saucepan. Stir in the peanut butter until smooth. Mixing continuously over low heat, add 1¾ c. (440 mL) water. Stir to keep smooth. When mixture simmers, add sugar, stirring until dissolved. Serve hot.

LYCHEE/SUGAR CANE DRINK WITH GINGER FLAVOR 薑花荔枝甘蔗汁

1 c.	sugar cane juice	250 mL
1 c.	lychee juice	250 mL
¼ t.	fresh ginger, grated (optional)	1 mL
1 t.	lemon juice, to taste	5 mL

Mix all ingredients; chill. Serve over ice.

MANDARIN ORANGE/SUGAR CANE FRUIT DRINK 甘蔗,橘子汁

1 c.	sugar cane juice	250 mL
1 c.	mandarin orange juice	250 mL
1 t.	lemon juice, to taste	5 mL
	ginger ale (optional)	

Mix all ingredients; chill. Serve over ice, with or without ginger ale.

REAL GINGER ALE 薑花汽水

1 c.	ginger ale	250 mL
⅛ t.	fresh ginger, grated	.5 mL
	cracked ice to fill 10-oz. (300-mL) glass	

Mix the ginger ale and ginger. Pour over ice and serve.

LYCHEE/LONGAN/MANDARIN ORANGE NECTAR　龍枝橘露

20-oz. can	lychees	565-g can
15-oz. can	longans	425-g can
11-oz. can	mandarin oranges	311-g can

Purée each fruit with its juice. Combine the fruit purées in a container; refrigerate 2 hours. Serve over ice.

Note: If desired, add Mandarine Napoléon or Grand Marnier liqueur, to taste, before refrigerating.

GINGER-LACED PINEAPPLE DRINK　薑花波羅露

1 c.	unsweetened pineapple juice	250 mL
⅛ t.	fresh ginger, grated	.5 mL

Mix juice and ginger thoroughly. Chill and serve.

LYCHEE NECTAR WITH RASPBERRY FLAVOR　紅山莓荔枝露

8½-oz. can	lychee nectar	241-g can
1 t.	seedless red raspberry jam	5 mL

Mix nectar and jam in a bowl. Chill. Serve over ice cubes or crushed ice.

LONGAN NECTAR WITH RASPBERRY FLAVOR　紅山莓龍眼露

	juice from 15-oz. (425-g) can longans	
1 t.	seedless red raspberry jam	5 mL

Mix juice and jam in a bowl. Serve over ice cubes or crushed or shaved ice.

Note: To make loquat nectar, substitute juice from a 15-oz. (425-g) can loquats for the longan juice.

MIXED CHINESE FRUIT PUNCH　什錦果汁

2 t.	lemon juice	10 mL
1 c.	lychee juice	250 mL
1 c.	longan juice	250 mL
1 c.	loquat juice	250 mL
drops	red food coloring	drops
	maraschino cherries	

Combine juices in a container. Add coloring; mix. Refrigerate for 1 hour. Serve in glasses over ice, garnished with cherries.

Note: For variety, you may substitute ½ c. (125 mL) mandarin orange juice for the longan juice and Grand Marnier liqueur for the lemon juice; or try combinations using pear, cherry, or rambutan juice for lychee, longan, or loquat juice.

LYCHEE/LOQUAT/MANDARIN ORANGE/ STRAWBERRY PUNCH　荔枝枇杷柑梅汁

20-oz. can	lychees	565-g can
15-oz. can	loquats	425-g can
11-oz. can	mandarin oranges	311-g can
10-oz. pkg	frozen strawberries	283-g pkg

Drain each fruit over a bowl; set aside fruits for another dish. Measure ½ c. (125 mL) each of lychee, loquat, and orange juice into a container; add ¼ c. (60 mL) strawberry juice. Refrigerate for 1 hour. Serve iced.

Note: Instead of the strawberry juice, you may prefer to substitute 2 t. (10 mL) Mandarine Napoléon or Grand Marnier liqueur.

FIVE DIFFERENT INGREDIENT PUNCH

½ c.	mandarin orange juice	125 mL
½ c.	loquat juice	125 mL
½ c.	pineapple juice	125 mL
½ c.	lychee juice	125 mL
¼ t.	lemon juice	1 mL

Mix all juices in blender; chill. Serve over ice cubes.

GINGER-PEACHY PUNCH

6-oz. can	peach nectar	170-g can
1 T.	ginger preserves	15 mL
¼ t.	lemon juice	1 mL
1/16 t.	fresh ginger, grated	.25 mL

Blend all ingredients. Chill and serve.

LYCHEE/MANDARIN ORANGE/STRAWBERRY PUNCH

20-oz. can	lychees	565-g can
11-oz. can	mandarin oranges	311-g can
10-oz. pkg.	frozen strawberries	283-g pkg.
2 t.	lemon juice	10 mL

Drain each fruit over a bowl; set aside fruits for another dish. Combine ¾ c. (190 mL) lychee juice, ½ c. (125 mL) orange juice and ¼ c. (60 mL) strawberry juice in a container; add lemon juice. Refrigerate for 1 hour. Serve chilled.

LYCHEE MELBA PUNCH

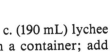

20-oz. can	lychees in syrup	565-g can
2 T.	black currant preserves	30 mL
2 T.	seedless red raspberry preserves	30 mL
½ t.	lemon juice	2 mL

Drain lychees over a bowl; whip the lychees in blender for 2 minutes. Stir in lychee juice and remaining ingredients. Serve chilled.

Note: Add 1 t. (5 mL) Mandarine Napoléon liqueur for additional flavor.

LYCHEE BLACKBERRY PUNCH WITH GINGER FLAVOR

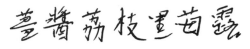

20-oz can	lychees in syrup	565-g can
2 T.	blackberry preserves	30 mL
2 t.	preserved ginger in syrup	10 mL
½ t.	lemon juice	2 mL

Drain lychees over bowl; whip the lychees in a blender for 2 minutes. Add lychee juice and remaining ingredients. Refrigerate until thoroughly chilled, then serve.

Note: For a variation, follow instructions above, adding 1 t. (5 mL) plum wine.

PINEAPPLE SUGAR CANE PUNCH

波萝甘蔗汁

1 c.	sugar cane juice	125 mL
1 c.	pineapple juice	125 mL
1 t.	lemon juice, to taste	5 mL

Mix all ingredients; chill. Serve over ice.

RAMBUTAN/LOQUAT/CHERRY PUNCH

丹櫻枇把露

⅓ c.	rambutan juice	90 mL
⅓ c.	cherry juice	90 mL
⅓ c.	loquat juice	90 mL
¼ t.	lemon juice	1 mL

Mix all ingredients in a large glass; chill. Serve iced.

Note: To make Lychee/Cherry/Pear Punch, substitute the same amount of lychee and pear juices for the rambutan and loquat juices and eliminate the lemon juice.

PLUM/BLACK CHERRY PUNCH

櫻桃李子汁

½ c.	black cherry soda	125 mL
1 T.	plum wine	15 mL
	cracked ice to fill	
	tall glass	

Mix soda and wine. Pour over ice and serve. Repeat recipe for each serving.

Note: For a variation, substitute 2 T. (30 mL) lychee juice for the wine to make Lychee/Black Cherry Punch.

RAMBUTAN/MANDARIN ORANGE/APRICOT DRINK

橘丹杏汁

¼ c.	rambutan juice	60 mL
⅛ c.	mandarin orange juice	30 mL
⅛ c.	apricot juice or nectar	30 mL
½ c.	water (optional)	125 mL

Mix ingredients well. Serve over ice.

Note: To make Rambutan/Mandarin Orange Fruit Punch, do not add the apricot juice or water.

BLENDED FRUIT PUNCHES

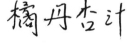

四色果汁

pineapple juice
apple juice
white grape juice
peach nectar

Delicious blends may be made by substituting 1 part pineapple, apple, white grape, or peach juice for a Chinese juice in the above punches. Serve chilled.

CHINESE FRUIT & SUGAR CANE PUNCH

甘蔗,橘子水

1 c.	sugar cane juice	250 mL
1 c.	mandarin orange juice	250 mL
1 c.	lychee juice	250 mL

| 1 t. | seedless red raspberry preserves | 5 mL |
| 1 t. | lemon juice, to taste | 5 mL |

Mix all ingredients; chill. Serve over ice.

LI-LY ROYAL PUNCH

灵根荔枝露

20-oz. can	lychees, drained	565-g can
3 T.	lingonberries in sugar	45 mL
½ t.	lemon juice	2 mL

Reserve lychees for a dessert. Mix lychee juice with sugar and lemon juice. Chill for 1 hour in refrigerator. Serve over ice.

SPARKLING LYCHEES WITH SPECIAL FLAVORS

特香汽醸荔枝

12 canned lychees, drained
black cherry soda or orange soda,
ginger ale, quinine water, club
soda

Place lychees in a bowl; cover with one of the suggested drinks. Cover bowl with plastic wrap; refrigerate for 1 hour. Serve in a glass with chopsticks to pick up the lychees.

Note: You may substitute longans or loquats for the lychees.

SWEET WINE ORANGES

酒醸橘子

1 c.	Sweet Rice Wine	250 mL
3–4 c.	boiling water	750 mL–1L
11-oz. can	mandarin oranges	311-g can

Mix wine and water in a saucepan. Bring to a boil. Add oranges and mix well. Serve hot in cups with chopsticks to eat the oranges.

FRUIT TEAS FOR DESSERT

果汁茶

instant tea or brewed Chinese tea
canned lychee juice
canned loquat juice
canned mandarin orange juice
canned longan juice
canned pineapple juice

Flavorful fruit teas may be made by mixing equal parts of your favorite tea with lychee, loquat, mandarin orange, or longan juice, or half pineapple juice with a Chinese juice. Try mixing your own blend. Serve hot or cold.

LYCHEE/LYCHEE BLACK TEA

荔枝茶荔枝

6 c.	water	1½ L
2 T.	lychee black tea leaves	30 mL
1 c.	canned lychee juice	250 mL
3 t.	lemon juice	15 mL
¼ c.	sugar	60 mL

Bring water to a boil in a saucepan. Remove from heat; add tea, stir for 15 seconds; cover and brew 5 minutes. In another small saucepan, mix juices and sugar; bring to a boil. Add brewed tea; strain and serve at once in teacups.

JASMINE LYCHEE TEA

6 c.	water	1½ L.
3 T.	jasmine tea leaves	45 mL
1 c.	canned lychee juice	250 mL
2 T.	lemon juice	30 mL
¼ c.	sugar	60 mL

香片檸枝茶

Bring water to a rolling boil in a saucepan; do not boil for a prolonged period. Remove from heat; add tea immediately. Stir for 15 seconds; cover and brew 5 minutes. In another small saucepan, mix juices and sugar and bring to a boil. Combine the 2 mixtures; strain and serve at once in teacups.

CHINESE ICED JASMINE TEA

茉莉花冷茶

3 T.	good grade jasmine or Earl Grey tea leaves	45 mL
4 c.	cold water	1 L

Place tea leaves in a 1-qt. (1-L) container; add water. Cover and refrigerate 8 to 24 hours. Strain tea. Serve cold over ice.

Note: Tea can also be prepared by this method with tea bags, if necessary, using 1 tea bag for each cup of water. Let stand at room temperature or refrigerate 6 to 8 hours.

RAMBUTAN/PEACH DESSERT/TEA

红毛丹桃子茶

20-oz. can	rambutans (or lychees)	565-g can
16-oz. can	sliced peaches	454-g can
¾ c.	sugar	190 mL
	water	
3 T.	plum wine	45 mL

Drain fruits in strainers over separate bowls; set aside the juices. Chop peaches into ¼-in. (6 mm) pieces or smaller. Combine the juices, adding enough water to make 4 c. (1 L). Bring sugar and water to a boil in a saucepan. Add the fruit and juices; simmer 2 minutes. Stir in the wine. Serve.

FOURTEEN PRECIOUS INGREDIENTS TEA

二七八宝茶

6 pieces	candied lotus root	6 pieces
6	preserved pitted kumquats	6
3 pieces	sweetened stem ginger, finely chopped	3 pieces
6 pieces	candied water chestnuts	6 pieces
6 pieces	candied winter melon	6 pieces
6	canned loquats, drained	6
6	canned lychees, drained	6
12 segments	canned mandarin oranges, drained	12 segments
½ c.	canned lychee juice	125 mL
½ c.	canned loquat juice	125 mL
½ c.	canned mandarin orange juice	125 mL
½ t.	lemon juice	2 mL
¼ t.	fresh ginger, grated	1 mL
1 t.	almond extract	5 mL

Cut the first 5 fruits into ¼-in. (6 mm) cubes. Cut the loquats, lychees, and oranges in half; mix all the fruits in a bowl. Place remaining ingredients except almond extract in a saucepan; bring to a boil. Add the fruits and simmer 2 minutes. Stir in the almond flavoring. Pour into a bowl. Chill in refrigerator for 2 hours. Serve in dessert dishes.

TRIPLE DELIGHT ICED TEA WITH ARBUTUS FLAVOR　　洋梅冰茶.

½ c.	arbutus juice	125 mL
½ t.	seedless red raspberry preserves	2 mL
½ c.	jasmine tea	125 mL

Mix all ingredients thoroughly. Chill and serve or pour over ice and serve.

JASMINE/LYCHEE TEA PUNCH　　茉莉荔枝汁

20-oz. can	lychees	565-g can
2 qt.	boiling water	2 L
3 T.	jasmine tea leaves	45 mL
	sugar, to taste	
1 T.	lemon juice (optional)	15 mL

Drain lychees over a bowl; set aside the juice. Pour water over the tea leaves; cover and brew 5 minutes. Strain tea into a container. Add sugar, to taste. Add lychee juice and lemon juice, if using. Pour over ice in a punch bowl.

OTHER TEA/FRUIT JUICE TEA PUNCHES　　各色茶.果汁

> *lychee juice with jasmine tea*
> *loquat juice with lychee black tea*
> *longan juice with rose tea*
> *arbutus juice with chinu black tea*
> *rambutan juice with keemun or oolong tea*
> *mandarin orange juice with keemun or oolong tea*

Follow directions for making Jasmine/Lychee Tea Punch, substituting desired tea and fruit juice. The amount of tea leaves can be adjusted to suit individual taste. Use all the juice in which the fruits have been packed. Although the above combinations are suggested, you may combine any fruit juice with any tea.

PINK LYCHEE-ADE　　粉红荔枝

20-oz. can	lychees	565-g can
2 c.	water	500 mL
1 t.	sugar	5 mL
2 T.	grenadine syrup	30 mL
	maraschino cherries (optional)	

Separate lychees from the juice; set aside the fruit for another dessert. Mix the juice with sugar and syrup. Serve over ice in small tumblers, garnished with 2 cherries, if using.

Note: For variety, substitute loquats, longans, or mandarin oranges for the lychees.

LYCHEE ICE CUBES　　荔枝冰塊

| 20-oz. can | lychees | 565-g can |
| 9 | maraschino cherries, cut in half | 9 |

Drain lychees over a bowl; pour the juice into an ice-cube tray. Place a lychee and a cherry half in each cube section of tray; freeze. Serve cubes in punch, fruit teas, and carbonated beverages.

Note: For tasty and attractive variations, instead of lychees and cherries, use longans with 1 t. (5 mL) lemon juice and a mandarin orange in each cube; use loquats with ½ pitted, preserved kumquat in each cube.

ICED KEEMUN TEA

祈门冰茶

4½ t.	keemun tea leaves	22 mL
2 c.	cold water	500 mL

Combine tea and water in a container; cover with lid. Refrigerate 8 hours (tea leaves will settle on the bottom of the container). Strain tea. Serve over ice.

KEEMUN TEA WITH LYCHEE FLAVOR

祈门荔枝茶

Add ½ c. (125 mL) lychee juice (reserved from another recipe) to the strained tea. Mix and serve.

ICED ROSE TEA

玫瑰冰茶

Follow directions for Iced Keemun Tea, substituting 4½ t. (22 mL) rose tea for keemun tea.

ICED ROSE TEA WITH LOQUAT FLAVOR

枇杷玫瑰冰茶

Add ½ c. (125 mL) canned loquat juice (reserved from another recipe) to the strained tea. Mix and serve.

LYCHEE PEACH TOFU COOLER

荔桃凍豆腐

8 oz.	tofu	225 g
1½ c.	frozen peaches	375 mL
2 t.	sugar	10 mL
1/16 t.	ground cinnamon	.25 mL
½ t.	lemon juice	2 mL
½ c.	canned lychee juice (reserved from another recipe)	125 mL
1	egg white	1

Mix all ingredients in blender until thoroughly blended. Refrigerate 1 hour. Serve over ice cubes as a beverage.

LYCHEE/PEACH FROSTED

轻鬆蛋白荔桃

1 c.	lychee juice	250 mL
1½ c.	frozen peaches	375 mL
1	egg white	1

Blend the ingredients until frothy and creamy. Serve chilled as a drink or in a sherbet cup with a spoon.

LYCHEE SHAKE

荔枝奶

20-oz. can	lychees	565-g can
1 t.	lemon juice	5 mL
½ c.	cold milk	125 mL
2 large scoops	vanilla ice cream	2 large scoops

Drain lychees over a bowl; set aside the juice. Purée lychees in a blender. Beat puréed lychees and remaining ingredients with ¼ c. (60 mL) lychee juice until thick. Serve in tall glasses.

Note: You may substitute loquats or longans for the lychees.

RICE WINE

米酒

Rice wine, a traditional and popular drink in China, is often served at major festivals, as postprandial dessert wine, or as a midnight snack. Sweet or glutinous rice is mixed with yeast to produce this fermented brew.

"Sweet rice wine" was discovered when the selected strain of yeast reacted with the water-soluble starch of the rice and formed sugar to make a very sweet and fragrant brew. When the yeast reacts further, the sugar is converted into alcohol. If the process is allowed to continue, rice vinegar is eventually formed. To preserve the brew at the wine stage, refrigerate after 4 or 5 days to stop the fermentation process and prevent the formation of vinegar.

SWEET RICE WINE

酒釀

4 c.	glutinous or sweet rice	1 L
¼ piece (1 t.)	Chinese yeast ball*	¼ piece (5 mL)
1 t.	all-purpose flour	5 mL

Soak rice in hot water for 1 hour. Drain water and steam rice for 25 minutes; rinse with warm water until rice is lukewarm. Combine the yeast and flour; add to the lukewarm rice, mixing well. Place the rice mixture in a 3-qt. (3-L) saucepan; make a well in middle and cover the pan with tightly stretched plastic wrap and lid of pan. Leave in slightly warm oven. Or wrap container with towel and leave it in a warm spot. After 4 to 5 days, mixture will have wine fragrance. Transfer to a jar and cover tightly.

Note: Wine can be kept for months in the refrigerator. Serve Sweet Rice Wine plain or diluted with water, to taste. To serve with water, bring water to a boil, add the wine and serve hot. Or, combine the wine with fruit. You may like the wine as a dessert dish prepared as egg drop soup with 1 egg. Beat the egg and slowly add the egg to the boiling wine in a steady stream. The egg will coagulate. Serve hot.

*A dried cultured yeast concentrate in the shape of a white ball is available at Chinese grocery stores.

MANDARIN ORANGE SWIZZLE

冰花橘子汽水

2 11-oz. cans	mandarin oranges	2 311-g cans
1 qt.	ginger ale, chilled	1 L
4 drops	yellow food coloring	4 drops
	maraschino cherries	

Drain the orange juice into a container; set aside the fruit segments. Chill the juice. When cold, add ginger ale and coloring. Pour over crushed ice or ice cubes in punch cups, garnished with cherries on toothpicks.

WATER CHESTNUT/SESAME BUTTER DRINK

馬蹄芝蔴糊

2 T.	water chestnut starch or cornstarch	30 mL
2 T.	water	30 mL
2 T.	sesame butter	30 mL
1¾ c.	water	440 mL
1–1½ c.	sugar	250–375 mL
pinch	salt	pinch

Combine starch and water in a qt. (L) saucepan; mix until smooth. Add sesame butter and stir until smooth. Mixing continuously over low heat, add the water, stirring to keep smooth. When the mixture simmers, season with sugar and salt. Serve hot.

SOYBEAN MILK

1 c.	soybeans	250 mL
8 c.	water	2 L
	salt or sugar, to taste	

Wash and clean the soybeans; cover with cold water and soak overnight; wash and drain. Place ¼ c. (60 mL) soaked soybeans in blender; add 1 c. (250 mL) water; grind for 1 minute at high speed. Add 1 c. (250 mL) more water and grind until very smooth, about 1 minute. Strain bean liquid slurry through a piece of cheesecloth. Squeeze out as much fine slurry as possible; repeat procedure until all soybeans have been processed. Place strained soybean slurry in a saucepan; cook over medium heat until it just simmers (do not boil); turn off heat. Serve hot or cold, sweetened with sugar. Soybean milk can be safely kept in refrigerator for a few days.

ALMOND DRINK

¼ c.	almond flour	60 mL
2 t.	water chestnut starch or cornstarch	10 mL
2 c.	milk	500 mL
1 c.	water	250 mL
2–3 t.	sugar, to taste	10–15 mL
dash	salt	dash

Place almond flour and starch in a 2-qt. (2-L) saucepan. Add a small amount of milk to make a paste. Stir until smooth. Add remaining milk and ingredients. Cook over low heat, stirring constantly. Simmer and stir until smooth. Serve hot.

Frozen Desserts

Frozen desserts — ice creams, sherbets, and ices — challenge the palate with their stimulating temperature, flavors, and textures. Complementing the heartier foods of earlier courses, frozen desserts melt in the mouth and effortlessly slide down, even for those who believe they could not swallow another bite.

Some Chinese restaurants outside China have customarily offered frozen desserts. Although they did not develop in the classic Chinese cuisine that emerged before refrigeration and freezing were possible, frozen desserts have certainly found acceptance and appreciation in modern times in countries all over the world, including China. Restaurateurs find these the easiest desserts to serve since they can be purchased in bulk commercially and require no preparation in a busy kitchen.

At home, ice cream, sherbets, and ices flavored with the traditional Chinese fruits can be served as very special and unusual treats, prepared in advance, and stored in the freezer for indefinite periods.

Some of the following recipes require no special equipment. If your family consumes huge quantities of ice cream, however, an ice cream maker may be a significant addition to the kitchen. It will contribute much to the table and to table talk when its products are served. Automatic, electric ice cream makers of many types are available, ranging from moderately expensive to quite expensive, based on the amount of labor they can perform. Among these are those manufactured by Simac (Il Gelatio 1600, and others), Gattia, and White Mountain.

These flavorful recipes have some differences: *Ice creams* are made with cream and milk from either a simple base or a creamier custard base; *sherbets* are made with milk; *ices* contain no dairy products.

Almost every recipe for frozen desserts calls for frequent stirring during the freezing process in order to break up the ice crystals that form. If an ice cream maker is not at hand for this part of the process, the techniques for making frozen desserts require only readily available kitchenware, frequently timed watch periods, and a little muscle power. When frozen desserts are eaten without having been stored for a long period in the freezer, they are of a somewhat less firm and creamier consistency.

To prepare frozen desserts without a mechanical ice cream maker, follow these instructions: Pour the mixture of ingredients into 9-in. (23-cm)-square cake pans or ice trays with the dividers removed. Cover with foil and place in freezer. When mixture becomes slushy, remove tray from freezer and beat briefly with a whisk to break up the ice crystals. Return covered tray to freezer and leave there until mixture is solid. Remove from freezer, break mixture into chunks and beat in a bowl with a rotary beater until creamy but not melted. Replace mixture in ice tray, cover, and return tray to freezer. When the ice cream is firm, it is ready to serve.

CUSTARD BASE (FOR ICE CREAM)　蛋奶冰淇淋李方

3 c.	heavy cream	750 mL
1 c.	milk	250 mL
¾ c.	sugar	190 mL
2	egg yolks	2

Combine cream, milk, and sugar in a heavy saucepan or double pan or double boiler; heat until warm and sugar is completely dissolved. Beat yolks until slightly creamy. Add 1 c. (250 mL) cream mixture to the yolks while whisking lightly. Pour into remaining cream mixture while continuing to whisk lightly. Cook over medium heat, stirring constantly, until back of spoon is thinly coated, about 8 minutes. (Do *not* allow it to boil or custard will curdle.) Cool and use in recipes that follow. Or freeze and use when ready to mix your special recipe. Makes 1 qt. (1 L) custard base.

Note: For a variation of this base, see Vanilla Ice Cream.

VANILLA ICE CREAM　香草冰淇淋

| 1 qt. | Custard Base | 1 L |
| 2 T. | vanilla extract | 30 mL |

Mix the base and vanilla. Freeze in ice cream maker or use freezer tray method.

Note: You may use this recipe as a base for other ice cream variations.

ALMOND ICE CREAM　杏仁冰淇淋

1 qt.	Custard Base	1 L
1 t.	almond extract	5 mL
½ c.	blanched almonds, chopped	125 mL

Mix all ingredients until well blended. Freeze in ice cream maker or use freezer tray method.

ALMOND-PEACH ICE CREAM　杏桃冰淇淋

2 20-oz. cans	Chinese white peaches or home-style canned peaches	2 565-g cans
1 qt.	Custard Base	1 L
1 t.	almond extract	5 mL

Drain peaches and set aside the juice for another dessert. Mash the peaches. Mix in the extract. Freeze in ice cream maker or use freezer tray method.

ARBUTUS ICE CREAM　洋梅冰淇淋

| 2 20-oz. | cans arbutus | 2 565-g cans |
| 1 qt. | Custard Base | 1 L |

Drain arbutus; set aside the juice for another dessert. Before mashing fruit, remove the pits. Mix fruit and base. Freeze in ice cream maker or use freezer tray method.

SIMPLE COCONUT ICE CREAM

椰子冰淇淋

15-oz. can	sweetened cream of coconut	425-g can
1½ c.	milk	375 mL
2 c.	heavy cream	500 mL
¾ c.	tightly packed, sweetened coconut, shredded	190 mL

Mix cream of coconut, milk, and heavy cream in blender. Stir in the coconut. Freeze in ice cream maker or use freezer tray method.

COINTREAU ICE CREAM

康酒冰淇淋

1 qt.	Custard Base	1 L
½ c.	Cointreau liqueur	125 mL

Mix base and liqueur. Freeze in ice cream maker or use freezer tray method.

Note: For variety, you may like the flavor of Mandarine Napoléon liqueur instead of the Cointreau.

DATE JAM ICE CREAM

枣蓉冰淇淋

1 qt.	Custard Base	1 L
1 c.	date jam	125 mL
3 T.	lemon juice	45 mL

Mix all ingredients in blender. Freeze in ice cream maker or use freezer tray method.

GINGER ICE CREAM

糖薑冰淇淋

1 qt.	Custard Base	1 L
½ c.	crystallized ginger, finely chopped	125 mL
¼ t.	ground ginger	1 mL

Mix all ingredients. Freeze in ice cream maker or use freezer tray method.

Note: You can substitute ½ c. (125 mL) ginger preserves for the crystallized ginger.

GINGER PEACH ICE CREAM

薑桃冰淇淋

2 20-oz. cans	Chinese white peaches or home-style canned peaches	2 565-g cans
1 qt.	Custard Base	1 L
3 T.	crystallized ginger, finely chopped	45 mL

Drain peaches; set aside the juice for another dessert. Mash peaches. Mix with the base and ginger. Freeze in ice cream maker or use freezer tray method.

Note: Instead of the crystallized ginger, flavor your ice cream with 3 T. (45 mL) ginger preserves.

GINGER PEAR ICE CREAM

薑梨冰淇淋

8	ripe pears, cored and peeled	8
4 T.	crystallized ginger, chopped	60 mL
4 T.	lemon juice	60 mL
1 qt.	Custard Base	1 L

Purée pears in blender with ginger and lemon juice. Add base and blend briefly. Freeze in ice cream maker or use freezer tray method.

LONGAN ICE CREAM

龍眼蛋奶冰淇淋

2 15-oz. cans	longans	2 425-g cans	
1 qt.	Custard Base	1 L	
3 T.	lemon juice	45 mL	

Drain longans; set aside the juice. Finely chop longans with a cleaver. Mix with the base and lemon juice. Freeze in ice cream maker or use freezer tray method.

LOQUAT ICE CREAM

枇杷蛋奶冰淇淋

2 15-oz. cans	loquats	2 425-g cans	
1 qt.	Custard Base	1 L	
3 T.	lemon juice	45 mL	

Drain loquats; set aside the juice for another dessert. Finely chop loquats with a cleaver. Mix with the base and lemon juice. Freeze in ice cream maker or use freezer tray method.

LYCHEE ICE CREAM

荔枝蛋奶冰淇淋

2 20-oz. cans	lychees	2 565-g cans	
1 qt.	Custard Base	1 L	
3 T.	lemon juice	45 mL	

Drain lychees; set aside the juice for another dessert. Finely chop lychees with a cleaver. Mix with base and lemon juice. Freeze in ice cream maker or use freezer tray method.

SIMPLE LYCHEE ICE CREAM

如意荔枝冰淇淋

2 20-oz. cans	lychees	2 565-g cans
¼ c.	sugar	60 mL
1 c.	heavy cream	250 mL
1 T.	lemon juice	15 mL

Drain the lychees; set aside ¾ c. (190 mL) of the juice. Purée lychees in a blender. Mix blended lychees, ¾ c. (190 mL) lychee juice and remaining ingredients in blender. Freeze in ice cream maker or use freezer tray method.

SIMPLE LYCHEE BANANA ICE CREAM

荔枝香蕉冰淇淋

2 20-oz. cans	lychees	2 565-g cans
2 small	ripe bananas	2 small
¼ c.	sugar	60 mL
1 c.	heavy cream	250 mL
2 T.	lemon juice	30 mL

Drain lychees; set aside ¾ c. (190 mL) of the juice. Purée lychees in blender. Add bananas; purée with the lychees. Add ¾ c. (190 mL) lychee juice and remaining ingredients to blender; blend well. Freeze in ice cream maker or use freezer tray method.

MANGO ICE CREAM

芒果冰淇淋

1 qt.	Custard Base	1 L	
2 15-oz. cans	sliced mangos, drained and coarsely chopped	2 425-g cans	
4 T.	lemon juice	60 mL	

Mix the base, mangos, and lemon juice. Freeze in ice cream maker or use freezer tray method.

MANDARIN ORANGE ICE CREAM

柑檬冰淇淋

1 qt.	Custard Base	1 L
2 11-oz. cans	mandarin oranges, drained and coarsely chopped	2 311-g cans
3 T.	lemon juice	45 mL

Mix all the ingredients. Freeze in ice cream maker or use freezer tray method.

Note: For a variation, add 2 t. (10 mL) vanilla extract and 3 T. (45 mL) Cointreau liqueur instead of the lemon juice.

MIDORI ICE CREAM

蜜多力冰淇淋

1 qt.	Custard Base	1 L
¾ c.	Midori melon liqueur	190 mL
	green food coloring (optional)	

Mix base, liqueur, and food coloring, if using. Freeze in ice cream maker or use freezer tray method.

PEACH ICE CREAM

桃子冰淇淋

2 20-oz. cans	Chinese white peaches or home-style canned peaches	2 565-g cans
1 qt.	Custard Base	1 L
2 t.	vanilla extract	10 mL

Drain and mash the peaches; set aside the juice for another dessert. Mix peaches with the base and lemon juice. Freeze in ice cream maker or use freezer tray method.

Note: To make Peach Coconut Ice Cream, follow the same directions, adding 1 c. (250 mL) sweetened shredded coconut instead of the vanilla.

PINEAPPLE ICE CREAM

波萝冰淇淋

2 20-oz. cans	crushed pineapple	2 565-g cans
1 qt.	Custard Base	1 L
	yellow food coloring	

Drain and purée 1 can pineapple in blender; set aside the pineapple juice for another dessert. Add base to blender; mix briefly. Pour mixture into a bowl; add coloring and remaining can of pineapple, as desired. Freeze in ice cream maker or use freezer method.

PISTACHIO ICE CREAM

必大渚冰淇淋

1 qt.	Custard Base	1 L
1 c.	shelled pistachio nuts, coarsely chopped	250 mL
½ t.	almond extract	2 mL
	green food coloring (optional)	

Mix the base, nuts, and flavoring. Color with drops of coloring, if desired. Freeze in ice cream maker or use freezer tray method.

PLUM WINE ICE CREAM

李酒冰淇淋

1 qt.	Custard Base	1 L
⅔ c.	plum wine	180 mL
12 drops	red food coloring (optional)	12 drops
8 drops	blue food coloring (optional)	8 drops

Mix the base, wine, and food coloring, if using. Freeze in ice cream maker or use freezer tray method.

RED BEAN PASTE ICE CREAM

红豆沙冰淇淋

1 qt.	Custard Base	1 L
1 c.	sweetened red bean paste	250 mL
3 T.	lemon juice	45 mL

Mix all ingredients in a blender. Freeze in ice cream maker or use freezer tray method.

Note: To make Banana Ice Cream, follow recipe above, substituting 2 mashed bananas for the red bean paste.

SIMPLE STRAWBERRY COCONUT ICE CREAM

草梅椰子冰淇淋

15-oz. can	sweetened cream of coconut	425-g can
1½ c.	milk	375 mL
2 c.	heavy cream	500 mL
2 c.	fresh strawberries, chopped	500 mL
¾ c.	sweetened shredded coconut, tightly packed	190 mL

Mix cream of coconut, milk, heavy cream, and strawberries in a blender. Stir in the coconut. Freeze in ice cream maker or use freezer tray method.

ALMOND PARFAIT

杏仁凍糕

2 c.	egg whites	500 mL
pinch	salt	pinch
⅓ c.	honey	90 mL
1 c.	heavy cream	250 mL
½ t.	almond extract	2 mL
2 T.	almonds, toasted and slivered	30 mL

Beat egg whites and salt in a small bowl until mixture holds a soft shape; continue beating, slowly pouring in honey until mixture forms stiff peaks. Whip cream and almond extract in a chilled bowl with chilled beaters until it holds a soft shape. Fold into the egg white mixture. Pour into large ice cube tray, serving bowl, or individual bowls. Cover and freeze until firm, about 4 to 5 hours. Sprinkle with almonds and serve.

Note: To use the reserved egg yolks, see Soft Egg Custard with Plum Wine.

LONGAN SHERBET

龍眼奶雪糕

15-oz. can	longans	425-g can
2 c.	milk	500 mL
¼ c.	sugar	60 mL
2 T.	lemon juice	30 mL

Drain longans and reserve the juice. Purée longans in blender. Mix the remaining ingredients and the longan juice with longans in the blender. Freeze in ice cream maker or use freezer tray method.

GINGER SHERBET

蕾花奶雪糕,

1 qt.	lemon sherbet	1 L
½ c.	dried crystalline ginger slices, very finely chopped	125 mL
¾ t.	fresh ginger, grated	4 mL

Allow sherbet to soften slightly. Mix the gingers into the sherbet. Refreeze, stirring often. Serve plain or with fruit.

LOQUAT SHERBET

枇杷奶雪糕,

15-oz. can	loquats	425-g can
2 c.	milk	500 mL
¼ c.	sugar	60 mL
2 T.	lemon juice	30 mL

Drain loquats over a bowl; set aside the juice. Purée loquats in blender. Add remaining ingredients to the loquats in the blender and mix. Freeze in ice cream maker or use freezer tray method.

MANGO SHERBET

芒果奶雪糕,

15-oz. can	sliced mangos	425-g can
2 c.	milk	500 mL
¼ c.	sugar	60 mL
2 T.	lemon juice	30 mL

Drain the mangos and set aside the juice. Purée mangos in blender. Mix in the remaining ingredients and the mango juice. Freeze in ice cream maker or use freezer tray method.

GINGER ICE

薑花冰

1½-in. piece	fresh ginger root	3.8-cm piece
½ c.	sugar	125 mL
2 c.	water	500 mL

Cut unpeeled ginger into thin slices and chop coarsely. In a saucepan, combine ginger, sugar, and water; cook for 5 minutes; cool. Freeze in ice cream maker or use freezer tray method.

LOQUAT ICE

枇杷冰

1 c.	water	250 mL
¼ c.	sugar	60 mL
15-oz. can	loquats	425-g can

Heat water and sugar in a saucepan until sugar dissolves. Drain loquats and set aside the juice. Purée loquats in blender. Add the syrup and juice to loquats in blender. Freeze in ice cream maker or use freezer tray method.

LYCHEE ICE

荔枝冰

15-oz. can	lychees	425-g can
1 t.	lemon juice	5 mL
	red food coloring (optional)	

Drain lychees and set aside the juice. Purée lychees in blender. Mix in the lemon and lychee juices; color, if desired. Freeze in ice cream maker or use freezer tray method.

LYCHEE SHERBET

荔枝奶雪糕

20-oz. can	lychees	565-g can
2 c.	milk	500 mL
¼ c.	sugar	60 mL
2 T.	lemon juice	30 mL

Drain the lychees and set aside the juice. Purée lychees in blender. Mix in the remaining ingredients and lychee juice. Freeze in ice cream maker or use freezer tray method.

Note: To make Midori Lychee Sherbet, follow directions above, adding 7 T. (105 mL) Midori liqueur with the flavorings.

MANDARIN ORANGE SHERBET

柑奶雪糕

11-oz. can	mandarin oranges	311-g can
2 c.	milk	500 mL
1 c.	sugar	250 mL
2 T.	lemon juice	30 mL

Drain the oranges and set aside the juice. Purée oranges in blender. Mix in the remaining ingredients and juice. Freeze in ice cream maker or use freezer tray method.

MANDARIN ORANGE/PINEAPPLE SHERBET

柑波蘿奶雪糕

11-oz. can	mandarin oranges, chilled	311-g can
20-oz. can	pineapple chunks, chilled	565-g can
2 c.	orange sherbet	500 mL

Drain oranges and pineapple and set aside their juices. Mix the fruits. Mix the juices. Fill sherbet glasses two-thirds full with the fruit mixture. Add a scoop of sherbet to each glass. Spoon 2 T. (30 mL) of the mixed juice over each portion.

MANDARIN ORANGE PEACH WHIP

柑桃凍

11-oz. can	mandarin oranges with the juice	311-g can
1½ c.	frozen peach segments	375 mL
2 t.	sugar	10 mL
½ t.	lemon juice	2 mL
2	egg whites	2

Place all ingredients in blender. Blend until frothy. Chill well. Serve in dessert cups.

MANDARIN ORANGE/LONGAN ICE

2 20 oz. cans	longans	2 565-g cans
11-oz. can	mandarin oranges	311-g can
1 c.	water	250 mL
¾ c.	sugar	190 mL
1 T.	lemon juice	15 mL

Drain longans and oranges; set aside their juices. Heat water and sugar in a saucepan until sugar dissolves. Add the lemon juice; cool. Mix syrup with fruit in blender. Freeze in ice cream maker or use freezer tray method.

Note: To make Midori Mandarin Orange/Longan Ice, follow directions above, adding 3 T. (45 mL) Midori liqueur with the syrup.

MANDARIN ORANGE SNOW

1 env.	unflavored gelatin	1 env.
¼ c.	cold water	60 mL
11-oz. can	mandarin oranges	311-g can
	orange juice or water (optional)	
4 T.	plum wine	60 mL
½ t.	vanilla extract	2 mL
¼ c.	sugar	60 mL
1	egg white	1

Soften gelatin in water; dissolve in a small saucepan over low heat, stirring constantly. Combine oranges and the juice, adding more juice or water to make 1 c. (250 mL) liquid, wine, vanilla, and sugar in blender; blend for 10 seconds. Beat egg white until stiff. Pour gelatin into a bowl; add the orange mixture and stir well. Fold in the beaten white; beat 30 seconds with egg beater. Chill in freezer or refrigerator until set. Serve in sherbet dishes.

GINGER SNOW

½ c.	cold water	125 mL
1 env.	unflavored gelatin	1 env.
¾ c.	sugar	190 mL
2 c.	sweetened coarse applesauce	500 mL
½ c.	ginger preserves	125 mL
6 T.	plum wine	90 mL
1 t.	lemon juice	5 mL
2 T.	Mandarine Napoléon or Grand Marnier liqueur	30 mL
2	egg whites	2

Pour water into a heavy saucepan; sprinkle the gelatin on top. Stir over low heat until gelatin dissolves; remove from heat and add the sugar, stirring until dissolved. Add the next 4 ingredients, mixing well. Chill until the mixture begins to gel, stirring occasionally. Stir in the liqueur and unbeaten whites. Beat with electric or hand rotary beater until mixture begins to become firm. Turn into a 2-qt. (2-L) mould or bowl. Chill until firm. Serve chilled.

Note: To make Kumquat Snow, follow directions for Ginger Snow, substituting ½ c. (125 mL) preserved kumquats, drained, seeded, and finely chopped, for the ginger preserves.

LYCHEE CHAMPAGNE SNOW

荔枝香檳雪

¾ c.	sugar	190 mL
¾ c.	water	190 mL
½ c.	canned lychee juice	125 mL
	juice of ½ lemon	
½ bottle	champagne, chilled	½ bottle
1	egg white, lightly beaten	1
1 drop	red food coloring	1 drop

Bring sugar, water, and lychee juice to a boil in uncovered saucepan; boil for 5 minutes. Add the coloring and lemon juice. Bring back to boil, then remove immediately from heat; cool. Pour cool syrup into large mixing bowl; stir in ½ the champagne; place bowl in freezer. As mixture begins to freeze, beat with wire whisk to break up crystals and produce a fluffy look. Then return to freezer; repeat this procedure several times. Add egg white and remaining champagne; return to freezer and remove occasionally and beat to maintain fluffiness. Chill individual stem glasses. Spoon the snow mixture into the chilled glasses and serve immediately.

ALMOND MARSHMALLOW WHIP

杏仁棉糖奶油凍

¼ lb.	marshmallows	120 g
1 c.	milk	250 mL
¼ c.	sugar	60 mL
1 c.	heavy cream	250 mL
1 T.	almond extract	15 mL
pinch	salt	pinch

Combine marshmallows, milk, and sugar. Cook over hot water until melted, stirring constantly. Cool until slightly thickened. Whip cream until slightly stiff. Add whipped cream, almond extract, and salt to the thickened marshmallow mixture; pour into ice tray. Freeze until firm.

CHINESE FRUIT SLUSH PARFAIT

枇杷荔枝凍糕,

20-oz. can	lychees	565-g can
15-oz. can	loquats	425-g can

Drain lychees and loquats over separate bowls; set aside their juices. Cut lychees in quarters; cut loquats in eighths. Combine lychees, loquats, and their juices in a bowl; mix well. Pour into freezer trays. Freeze until slushy, stirring once. Serve chilled in parfait or sherbet glasses.

ALMOND COOKIE ICE CREAM SANDWICHES 杏仁雪糕三文治

1 pt. (2 c.)	vanilla or almond ice cream	500 mL
16 large	almond cookies	16 large

Remove ice cream from freezer; let stand until slightly soft. Spread ½ c. (125 mL) ice cream on 1 cookie; place another cookie firmly on top. Repeat until all cookies are used. Wrap individually in plastic wrap. Return sandwiches to freezer until firm.

Ambrosias

MIXED CHINESE AMBROSIA

美味雜拌.

2 11-oz. cans	mandarin oranges	2 311-g cans
2	ripe bananas	2
1	apple	1
¼ c.	confectioners' sugar	60 mL
1½ c.	shredded coconut	375 mL

Drain the oranges; reserve the juice for another dessert. Thinly slice the bananas. Peel, core, and thinly slice the apple. Mix the sugar and coconut. Arrange alternate layers of oranges, banana and apple slices in individual serving dishes or a bowl. Sprinkle each layer with the coconut mixture; reserving some for the top. Chill well before serving.

PINEAPPLE AMBROSIA

芬香波羅

¾ c.	fresh pineapple, diced, or canned pineapple chunks, drained	190 mL
1½ 11-oz. cans	mandarin oranges, drained	1½ 311-g cans
⅓ c.	sugar	90 mL
⅔ c.	shredded or flaked coconut	180 mL

Alternate layers of pineapple and oranges in a serving bowl, sprinkling each layer with sugar and coconut. Chill for 1 hour before serving.

MANDARIN ORANGE AMBROSIA

椰香橘子

3 11-oz. cans	mandarin oranges	3 311-g cans
⅓ c.	sugar	90 mL
⅔ c.	shredded or flaked coconut, coarsely chopped	180 mL

Drain oranges; set aside the juice for another dessert. Arrange oranges in several layers in a serving bowl, sprinkling each layer with sugar and coconut. Chill for 1 hour.

PINEAPPLE/PLUM WINE AMBROSIA

椰絲李酒波蔓

20-oz. can	pineapple chunks	565-g can
3 T.	plum wine	45 mL
½ c.	shredded coconut	125 mL

Drain pineapple chunks; set aside the juice for another recipe. Chill the pineapple. Add the wine, mixing well. Place in a serving dish; stir in the coconut, mixing thoroughly.

STRAWBERRY AMBROSIA

椰香草梅

10-oz. pkg.	frozen sliced strawberries, thawed	283-g pkg.
2 11-oz. cans	mandarin oranges, drained	2 311-g cans
½ c.	shredded or flaked coconut	125 mL

Mix strawberry slices, oranges, and coconut. Arrange in layers in a serving bowl. Chill for 30 minutes.

BANANA AMBROSIA

芳香椰絲蕉

2	ripe bananas	2
11-oz. can	mandarin oranges, drained	311-g can
⅓ c.	sugar	90 mL
⅔ c.	shredded or flaked coconut	180 mL

Peel and slice bananas into ¼-in. (6-mm)-thick slices. In a serving bowl, alternate slices of bananas and oranges, sprinkling each layer with sugar and coconut. Chill for 1 hour before serving.

Baked, Broiled & Stir-Fried Fruits

BAKED LYCHEES

白塔蛋烤荔枝

½ c.	butter	125 mL
¾ c.	sugar	190 mL
5	egg yolks	5
¼ c.	dry bread crumbs	60 mL
20-oz. can	lychees, drained	565-g can
1 T.	lemon juice	15 mL
3	egg whites	3
2 T.	plum wine	30 mL
	nondairy whipped topping (optional)	

Cream the butter and sugar. In another bowl, mix the yolks, bread crumbs, lychees, and lemon juice. Beat into the creamed butter and sugar. Beat the egg whites until stiff; fold whites into the batter. Add the wine. Pour batter into a lightly greased baking dish. Set the dish in a pan of hot water and bake at 325 °F (165 °C) for 30 minutes. Serve hot or warm with topping, if desired.

Note: Baked Longans can be made by substituting a 15-oz. (425-g) can of longans for the lychees.

BAKED APPLES WITH CHINESE DATE FLAVOR

枣蓉烤苹果

6	baking apples, unpeeled	6
8 t.	date jam	40 mL
¼ t.	fresh ginger, grated	1 mL

Cut apples in half lengthwise; remove central core and seeds. Place 1 t. (5 mL) jam into each apple cavity; spread remaining jam over cut surface of the apples. Sprinkle ginger in middle of each. Arrange apples in square baking pan. Bake at 300 °F (150 °C) for 20 minutes. Serve warm or cold.

BAKED LYCHEES WITH LIQUEUR 甜酒烤荔枝

⅜ c.	sugar	90 mL
⅜ c.	water	90 mL
¼ t.	ground cinnamon	1 mL
1 T.	Mandarine Napoléon liqueur	15 mL
1 t.	butter	5 mL
20-oz. can	lychees, drained	565-g can

Mix sugar, water, and cinnamon in a saucepan; bring to a boil over high heat and simmer gently for 10 minutes. Stir in the liqueur. Remove from heat; mix in the butter. Place drained lychees in a baking dish, reserving the liquid for another use. Pour syrup over lychees. Cover with lid or aluminum foil. Bake at 350 °F (175 °C) for 10 minutes, basting several times. Serve hot.

Note: If desired, longans, rambutans, or loquats can be substituted for lychees.

BAKED TANGERINES WITH CHINESE DATE FLAVOR 枣蓉烤橘子

3	tangerines	3
8 t.	date jam	40 mL
¼ t.	fresh ginger, grated	1 mL

Cut tangerines in half crosswise; remove core and pits with serrated citrus knife. Place 1 t. (5 mL) jam into each tangerine cavity; spread jam over cut surface of the tangerines. Sprinkle ginger over each tangerine half. Arrange tangerines in a square baking pan. Bake at 300 °F (150 °C) for 20 minutes. Serve hot.

Note: For a variation, try this recipe with oranges or green pears instead of the tangerines.

BAKED GRAPEFRUIT WITH CHINESE DATE FLAVOR 枣蓉烤柚子

3	grapefruit	3
15 t.	date jam	75 mL
¼ t.	fresh ginger, grated	1 mL

Cut grapefruit in half crosswise; remove core and seeds with serrated citrus knife. Place 2 to 3 t. (10 to 15 mL) jam into cavity of each grapefruit half; spread more jam over cut surface. Sprinkle ginger in cavity of each grapefruit half. Arrange fruit in a baking pan. Bake at 300 °F (150 °C) for 20 minutes. Serve warm.

BROILED LYCHEES 烤荔枝

20-oz. can	lychees	565-g can
	sugar	
	margarine	
	ground cinnamon	

Drain lychees; set aside the juice for another recipe. Place lychees on a cookie sheet or square pan. Sprinkle sugar on each lychee; dot each lychee with margarine. Sprinkle with cinnamon. Brown under high heat in a broiler for 8 minutes. Serve at once.

Note: To make Broiled Loquat with Mandarine Napoléon Flavor, substitute canned loquats for lychees in the above recipe; add 2 drops Mandarine Napoléon liqueur to each fruit. Or, to prepare Broiled Longans, substitute canned longans for the lychees.

CHINESE STIR-FRIED STRAWBERRIES
WITH KUMQUAT

草梅炒金橘

½ c.	fresh strawberries, sliced in half	125 mL
1	preserved kumquat, pitted, finely chopped	1
¼ t.	lemon juice	1 mL
¹/₁₆ t.	fresh ginger, grated	¼ mL
½ t.	Mandarine Napoléon or Grand Marnier liqueur	2 mL
1 T.	water	15 mL
1 t.	peanut oil	5 mL

Mix the strawberries, kumquat, lemon juice, and ginger. In a cup, combine the liqueur and water. Heat the oil to the smoking point in a wok; add the strawberry mixture and stir-fry for 2 minutes. Pour into a bowl; stir in the liqueur mixture. Serve hot.

CHINESE STIR-FRIED NECTARINE

炒油桃

1	large nectarine, peeled and sliced in ¼-in. (6-mm) segments	1
2 t.	ginger preserves	10 mL
¼ t.	lemon juice	1 mL
¹/₁₆ t.	fresh ginger, grated	¼ mL
1 t.	sugar	5 mL
2 t.	Mandarine Napoléon or Grand Marnier liqueur	10 mL
1 T.	water	15 mL
2 T.	peanut oil	30 mL

Mix the first 5 ingredients. In a cup, mix the liqueur and water. Heat oil to the smoking point in a wok; add the fruit mixture and stir-fry for 2 minutes. Pour into a bowl; stir in the liqueur mixture. Serve hot.

Note: For a delicious variation, use either a large pear, apple, or peach instead of the nectarine.

Fruit Compotes & Salads

HOT CHINESE COMPOTE I

杏橘龍櫻热果、

17-oz. can	apricots	482-g can
11-oz. can	mandarin oranges	311-g can
15-oz. can	longans	425-g can
15	maraschino cherries	15
1 T.	maraschino cherry juice	15 mL
1 t.	fresh ginger, grated	5 mL

Drain the fruits over bowls and save the juices. Mix the fruits in an ovenware dish. Mix ⅓ c. (90 mL) *each* of the apricot, orange, and longan juices. Add the cherry juice. Pour the juices into the fruit mixture; add the ginger. Bake at 300 °F (150 °C) for 30 minutes. Serve hot in dessert dishes.

Note: To make Hot Chinese Compote with Plum Wine, slowly add ¼ c. (60 mL) plum wine, more or less to taste, just before serving.

HOT CHINESE COMPOTE II

薑花甜酸果

15-oz. can	loquats	425-g can
11-oz. can	mandarin oranges	311-g can
20-oz. can	rambutans	565-g can
8	maraschino cherries, halved	8
½ t.	fresh ginger, grated	2 mL
1 t.	lemon juice	5 mL
2 T.	sugar	30 mL
3 T.	plum wine (optional)	45 mL

Drain the fruits over bowls and save the juices. Mix the loquats, oranges, and rambutans in an ovenware dish. Combine the drained juices, measure 1 c. (250 mL) and pour over the fruit. Add the cherries. In a cup, mix the ginger, lemon juice, and sugar and stir into the fruit. Bake at 300 °F (150 °C) for 30 minutes. Add the wine, if desired, stirring gently. Serve hot.

Note: To prepare Hot Longan/Lychee/Peach Compote, use longans instead of the loquats, lychees instead of rambutans, and sliced peaches instead of mandarin oranges.

CHINESE FRUIT COCKTAIL

中式鸡尾果

30-oz. can	fruit cocktail	850-g can
2 T.	maraschino cherry juice	30 mL
10	maraschino cherries, sliced in half	10
½ c.	sweet white preserved cucumbers, coarsely chopped	125 mL
1 t.	almond extract	5 mL

Mix all the ingredients. Chill and serve.

Note: To serve Very Special Chinese Fruit Cocktail, prepare recipe as above; add 1 t. (5 mL) plum wine to the mixture before serving.

GINGER FRUIT COMPOTE

薑醬鮮果盅

11-oz. can	mandarin oranges	311-g can
1	apple, peeled, cut in cubes	1
1	banana, peeled, cut in ¼-in. (6-mm) slices	1
¼ t.	fresh ginger, grated	1 mL
¼ c.	canned lychee juice (reserved from another recipe)	60 mL
1 T.	ginger preserves	15 mL

Drain the oranges and save the juice. Mix all ingredients in a serving bowl. Refrigerate for 45 minutes. Serve chilled.

Note: For another dessert, Ginger Fruit Compote with Mandarine Napoléon Flavor, add 1½ t. (7 mL) Mandarine Napoléon or Grand Marnier liqueur to the above recipe.

ARBUTUS/LOQUAT DELIGHT

洋梅枇杷果

20-oz. can	arbutus	565-g can
15-oz. can	loquats	425-g can
1 t.	sugar	5 mL
¼ t.	lemon juice	1 mL
⅛ t.	fresh ginger, grated	.5 mL

Drain arbutus and loquats over separate bowls. Set aside half the arbutus for another dish and save the juice. Cut arbutus into small pieces and discard the pits. Reserve half the loquats for another dessert. In a bowl, mix the arbutus, loquats, one-third the arbutus juice and half the loquat juice. Add the lemon juice and ginger and stir well. Refrigerate for 1 hour. Serve chilled.

Note: To make Arbutus/Lychee Delight, follow directions above, substituting lychees for the loquats. Or, to serve Arbutus/Loquat Delight with Plum Wine Flavor, add 3 T. (45 mL) plum wine or 2 t. (10 mL) Mandarine Napoléon or Grand Marnier liqueur before refrigerating.

ARBUTUS COMPOTE

橘醬洋梅

20-oz. can	arbutus	565-g can
⅛ t.	fresh ginger, grated	.5 mL
1 T.	orange marmalade	15 mL
¼ t.	lemon juice	1 mL

Drain the fruit over a bowl; set aside the juice for another dessert. Combine arbutus and remaining ingredients in a bowl, mixing thoroughly. Marinate in refrigerator for 2 hours.

HOT LYCHEE COMPOTE

热汁荔枝

20-oz. can	lychees	565-g can
4	large preserved kumquats, pitted and cut in quarters	4
1 T.	kumquat syrup	15 mL
1 t.	lemon juice	5 mL
¼ c.	pineapple juice	60 mL

Mix all ingredients in a saucepan. Bring to a boil and simmer for 3 minutes. Serve hot.

Note: To make Hot Lychee Compote with Liqueur, follow directions for Hot Lychee Compote, adding 2 t. (10 mL) Mandarine Napoléon or Grand Marnier liqueur before serving.

LYCHEE LIQUEUR COMPOTE

李白荔枝

20-oz. can	lychees	565-g can
¾ c.	sugar	190 mL
⅛ t.	ground cinnamon	.5 mL
1 T.	ginger brandy	15 mL
2 T.	Mandarine Napoléon or Grand Marnier liqueur, to taste	30 mL

Drain the lychees and reserve the juice. Combine the juice, sugar, and cinnamon in a saucepan. Simmer for 5 minutes. Add lychees and simmer for an additional 2 minutes. With a slotted spoon, transfer the lychees to individual glass compotes or bowls. Boil the syrup a few minutes or until slightly thickened; remove from heat. Stir in the brandy and liqueur. Pour syrup over the lychees and serve warm.

LEMON COUPE WITH LONGANS, CHINESE STYLE

李酒金龍奶糕,

15-oz. can	longans	425-g can
9 T.	plum wine	135 mL
6 T.	preserved kumquats, finely minced	90 mL
2 c.	lemon ice or sherbet	500 mL

Drain longans and reserve 3 T. (45 mL) of the juice; cut longans in quarters. Mix the longans, reserved juice, wine, and kumquats in a bowl. Marinate for 1 hour in the refrigerator. Serve over scoops of lemon ice in sherbet dishes.

Note: To make Orange Coupe with Loquats, Chinese Style, substitute 2 c. (500 mL) orange ice or sherbet for the lemon ice and a 15-oz. (425-g) can loquats for the longans. Or, to serve Raspberry Coupe with Lychees, Chinese Style, substitute 2 c. (500 mL) raspberry ice or sherbet for lemon ice and a 20-oz. (565-g) can lychees for the longans.

FRUIT FONDUE

果子火鍋

⅔ c.	all-purpose flour	180 mL
2 T.	sugar	30 mL
1 T.	cornstarch	15 mL
½ t.	baking powder	2 mL
½ t.	salt	2 mL
½ c.	milk	125 mL
1	egg	1
	peanut oil for deep frying	
2	bananas, peeled and cut in ⅔-in. (8-mm) pieces	2
2 cans	lychees, loquats, and/or longans	2
2	apples, cored and sliced	2
2	peaches, pitted and sliced	2
2	pears, cored and diced	2
1 recipe	Fondue Warm Sauce	1 recipe

To make a batter, combine the first 7 ingredients in a bowl; beat mixture until smooth. Pour into a small serving bowl. Heat oil in a fondue pot to 365 °F (184 °C). Pick up a piece of fruit with chopsticks; dip in batter and drain off excess. Hold in hot oil until golden brown. Dip into Warm Sauce and eat.

Note: Guests can prepare their own servings.

MANDARIN ORANGE/MELBA COMPOTE

梅尔巴柑果醬

11-oz. can	mandarin oranges, including juice	311-g can
2 T.	ginger preserves	30 mL
1 T.	seedless red raspberry preserves	15 mL
1 T.	red currant jelly	15 mL
¼ t.	fresh ginger, grated	1 mL

Mix together all the ingredients in a saucepan. Heat until the mixture simmers. Serve warm.

PEARS WITH KUMQUAT & GINGER

薑花柑橘梨

16-oz. can	Bartlett pear halves	454-g can
6	preserved kumquats, pitted	6
¼ t.	fresh ginger, grated	1 mL
1 t.	fresh lemon juice	5 mL
1 T.	sugar	15 mL
½ c.	canned lychee juice (reserved from another recipe)	125 mL
½ c.	plum wine	125 mL

Drain the pears and set aside the juice. Cut pears into quarters. Coarsely chop the kumquats and place in a bowl. Mix in the remaining ingredients. Add the pears and marinate for 2 hours in the refrigerator. Serve chilled.

Note: To prepare Ginger Pears, follow recipe above, eliminating kumquats and plum wine.

LOQUAT COMPOTE

泗香枇杷

7.5 oz. can	loquats	210-g can
⅓ c.	plum wine	90 mL
1 T.	Mandarine Napoléon liqueur or Grand Marnier	15 mL
½ T.	blanched almonds, chopped (optional)	7.5 mL

Drain the loquats and reserve the juice. Add wine to the loquats; marinate for 15 minutes. Pour the juice into a saucepan; heat to the boiling point and boil to reduce to half the volume. Combine the marinated fruit with the juice; add the liqueur, stirring well. Add almonds, if using. Serve warm or cold.

KUMQUAT/MANDARIN ORANGES

枇杷柑甜美

11-oz. can	mandarin oranges	311-g can
6	kumquats, preserved in syrup	6
2 t.	preserved kumquat syrup	10 mL
1 t.	stem ginger, preserved in syrup	5 mL

Finely chop the oranges. Remove pits from the kumquats and finely chop them. Mix kumquats and all remaining ingredients in a bowl. Refrigerate 30 minutes or longer. Serve chilled.

CHILLED GINGER/PINEAPPLE COMPOTE

薑醬金橘波蘿

20-oz. can	unsweetened pineapple chunks	565-g can
2 T.	ginger preserves	30 mL
¼ t.	fresh ginger, grated	1 mL
1 T.	preserved kumquat syrup	15 mL

Mix all the ingredients thoroughly. Refrigerate for 2 hours. Serve chilled.

LI-LY COMPOTE

荔枝甜美

20-oz. can	lychees	565-g can
3 T.	lingonberries in sugar	45 mL
½ t.	lemon juice	2 mL
1 T.	sweet white preserved cucumber, very finely chopped	15 mL

Mix thoroughly the lychees, lingonberries, and lemon juice; add the cucumber, mixing well. Chill and serve in dessert dishes.

Fruits with Special Flavors

THE GINGERED PEACH

三薑桃

2 medium	peaches, cut in ¼-in. (6-mm) wedges	2 medium
2 t.	ginger preserves	10 mL
⅛ t.	fresh ginger, grated	.5 mL
2 t.	sugar	10 mL
2 T.	ginger ale	30 mL

Arrange peaches on a serving dish. Mix the remaining ingredients and spread over the peaches.

Note: You can use a medium apple, 1 c. (250 mL) seedless grapes, 2 large nectarines, 1 large pear, or 1⅓ c. (340 mL) fresh strawberries, cut in half, instead of the peaches.

LYCHEES WITH ARBUTUS FLAVOR

楊梅荔枝

16	lychees	16
⅔ c.	arbutus juice	180 mL
1 T.	sweet preserved white cucumber, finely chopped	15 mL

Mix all ingredients in a bowl; refrigerate. Serve chilled.

LONGANS & RASPBERRIES
WITH GINGER & ALMOND FLAVOR

杏仁薑酒龍莓

15-oz. can	longans with juice	425-g can
1 pkg.	frozen raspberries, defrosted	1 pkg.
6 T.	sugar	90 mL
1 T.	lemon juice	15 mL
¼ t.	fresh ginger, grated	1 mL
2 T.	ginger brandy, Mandarine Napoléon liqueur, or other fruit liqueur	30 mL
	slivered almonds	

Combine longans, raspberries, sugar, juice, and ginger in a serving bowl. Refrigerate until chilled. Add brandy and mix well. Serve with almonds sprinkled over each compote serving.

THREE DIFFERENT INGREDIENT KIWIS

三味人心果

2	kiwis, peeled, cut into ⅛-in. (3-mm)-thick slices	2
1 T.	orange marmalade	15 mL
¹⁄₁₆ t.	fresh ginger, grated	.25 mL
¼ t.	lemon juice	1 mL

Cut kiwi slices in half; place on a serving plate. Mix remaining ingredients and spread on the kiwis.

Note: Try using 2 large peaches instead of the kiwis for another combination.

NECTARINE WITH KUMQUAT FLAVOR

金橘油桃

2 large	nectarines, cut into ¼-in. (6-mm) wedges	2 large
1 T.	preserved kumquat syrup	15 mL

Cut nectarine wedges in half; marinate in the syrup. Chill and serve.

Note: Instead of the nectarines, use 1 large apple, peeled, cored and cut into wedges, 2 kiwis, peeled and sliced, or 2 large peaches, cut into ¼-in. (6-mm) wedges.

CANTALOUPE WITH TWO CHINESE FLAVORS

两香金瓜

2-in. section	cantaloupe, cut in wedges, bite-sized thin	5.1-cm section
2 T.	syrup of preserved kumquats	30 mL
¹⁄₁₆ t.	fresh ginger, grated	.25 mL

Place cantaloupe wedges in a dessert dish. Mix the syrup and ginger; add to the cantaloupe. Chill and serve.

Note: You may substitute casaba, cranshaw, honeydew, or Persian melon for the cantaloupe.

LOQUATS STUFFED WITH LONGANS

枇杷釀龍眼

15-oz. can	loquats	425-g can
20-oz. can	longans	565-g can
2 T.	Mandarine Napoléon or Grand Marnier liqueur	30 mL

Drain loquats and longans and reserve the juice. Coarsely chop the longans. Stuff a portion of the longans into the loquats; place on a serving dish. With a teaspoon or medicine dropper add 2 drops of liqueur into opening of the loquat. Chill and serve.

DATED STRAWBERRIES

枣蓉草梅

20	strawberries, cut in half	20
	date jam	

Place strawberries on a serving dish. Spoon jam on top of cut surface. Serve with toothpicks.

SPECIAL-FLAVORED CHINESE FRUIT

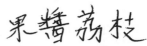

Canned lychees, drained, can be stuffed with the following: black currant preserves, damson plum preserves, duck sauce, raspberry preserves, red currant jelly, or sweet and sour sauce.

Canned longans, drained, can be stuffed with the following: black currant preserves, damson plum preserves, duck sauce, raspberry preserves, red currant jelly, or sweet and sour sauce.

Canned loquats, drained, can be stuffed with the following: black currant preserves, damson plum preserves, raspberry preserves, red currant jelly, or sweet and sour sauce.

Canned rambutans, drained, can be stuffed with the following: black currant preserves, damson plum preserves, duck sauce, raspberry preserves, red currant jelly, or sweet and sour sauce.

BLUSHING LYCHEES

2 20-oz. cans	lychees	2 565-g cans
½ c.	sugar	125 mL
4 T.	currant jelly	60 mL
1 T.	lemon juice	15 mL
1½ t.	lemon rind, grated	7 mL

Drain lychees; set aside the lychees. Mix 1 c. (250 mL) of the juice with sugar, jelly, lemon juice, and grated rind in a saucepan. Cover and simmer for 5 minutes until jelly dissolves. Add lychees; simmer 2 minutes. Remove from heat; let stand 8 minutes. With chopsticks, transfer lychees from syrup to a bowl. Cook syrup, stirring constantly, until it begins to thicken. Pour syrup mixture over lychees. Serve hot.

GINGER/PURPLE PLUMS

16-oz. can	purple plums	454-g can
⅛ t.	fresh ginger, grated	.5 mL
1 T.	sweet preserved white cucumber, coarsely chopped	15 mL
1 T.	ginger marmalade	15 mL

Place plums in a bowl. In a cup, thoroughly mix the remaining ingredients and add to the plums; mix well. Chill and serve.

SWEET PRESERVED PEARS
WITH LINGONBERRIES

20 pieces	sweet preserved pears, individually wrapped	20 pieces
2 T.	lingonberries in sugar	30 mL
¼ t.	lemon juice	1 mL
2–3 T.	water	30–45 mL

Unwrap the pear pieces; mix well with the remaining ingredients. Refrigerate for 2 hours or longer. Serve chilled in dessert glasses.

MANDARIN ORANGE PEACHES

香甜柑桃

15-oz. can	Korean white peach halves or same amount of country-style peach halves	425-g can
11-oz. can	mandarin oranges	311-g can
¼ c.	granulated brown sugar	60 mL
1½ t.	cornstarch	7 mL
¼ c.	orange marmalade	60 mL
pinch	salt	pinch
2½ T.	Mandarine Napoléon or Grand Marnier liqueur	37.5 mL

Drain peaches and oranges over separate bowls; reserve juices. Process oranges in blender until smooth. Combine orange juice with remaining ingredients in a saucepan. Gradually heat, adding reserved peach juice and puréed oranges. Bring mixture to a boil, stirring constantly. Add peaches; simmer 5 minutes, turning peaches several times; add the liqueur. Serve warm or chilled.

MANDARIN ORANGES WITH GINGER

薑花橘子

11-oz. can	mandarin oranges	311-g can
¼ t.	fresh ginger, grated	1 mL

In a bowl, combine the oranges and ginger; mix well. Refrigerate 30 minutes or longer. Serve chilled.

Note: To make Mandarin Oranges with Ginger & Liqueur, add ½ t. (2 mL) Mandarine Napoléon liqueur with the ginger.

GINGER/APPLE DESSERT CONSERVE

薑花苹果

3 c.	chunky applesauce	750 mL
1 t.	fresh ginger, grated	5 mL
1 t.	lemon juice	5 mL

Mix all ingredients and refrigerate for 1 hour. Serve as a spread for cake or add to fruit or custard cups.

LYCHEE/CHERRY MELANGE

什錦荔枝櫻桃

Follow directions for Lychee/Cherry Pie, eliminating Sweet Piecrust and all cooking. Serve cold in dessert bowls. Top with nondairy whipped topping, if desired.

Note: You may use blueberry or apple pie filling instead of cherries in the same recipe. Drizzle the mélange with ¼ t. (1 mL) Mandarine Napoléon or Grand Marnier liqueur instead of the plum wine, if you wish. For Chinese Mixed Fruit Mélange with Liqueur, follow directions for the above mélange, substituting longans, loquats, or rambutans for the suggested fruit, adding liqueur instead of wine.

ALMOND PEACHES

杏仁桃

16-oz. can	home-style peach halves	454-g can
¾ t.	almond extract	4 mL
⅛ t.	fresh ginger, grated	.5 mL
½ t.	lemon juice	2 mL

Chill peaches; drain over a bowl. Add almond extract to the juice; taste and add more, if desired. Add lemon juice. Place peaches in a dessert bowl. Dot the middle of each peach with ginger. Cover with the juice mixture. Chill and serve.

Note: For more ginger flavor, make Almond Peaches with Ginger Brandy. Follow recipe above, adding 2 t. (10 mL) ginger brandy to the juice.

LYCHEES CANTONESE

廣式荔枝

20-oz. can	lychees	565-g can
¼ c.	vinegar	60 mL
⅛ t.	ground cinnamon, more to taste	.5 mL
¼ c.	fresh ginger, cut in ⅛-in. (3-mm)-thick slices	60 mL

Drain lychees and pour the juice into a saucepan. Heat juice until it simmers for 30 seconds. Add vinegar, cinnamon, and ginger; simmer 4 minutes. Add lychees. Remove from heat at once; cool lychees in the liquid for 1 hour; remove ginger. Serve lychees in the liquid, warm or cold.

BLACK CHERRY LYCHEES

黑櫻枝

20-oz. can	lychees, chilled	565-g can
2 c.	black cherry soda	500 mL
2 T.	ginger preserves	30 mL
2 T.	sugar	30 mL

Drain lychees over a bowl; set aside the juice for another dessert. Pour soda into a large bowl; add lychees, preserves, and sugar. Refrigerate for 2 hours. Each serving should contain lychees and enough soda to cover fruit. Serve thoroughly chilled in sherbet glasses.

SPECIALLY SWEET AROMATIC LYCHEES

特香荔枝

1 T.	orange marmalade	15 mL
2 T.	currant jelly	30 mL
10	lychees	10

Mix the marmalade and jelly. Stir in the lychees; chill and serve.

Fruits with Liqueur & Wine

FLAMBÉED LYCHEES WITH GINGER BRANDY 薑酒耀日枷枝

½ c.	orange marmalade	125 mL
3 T.	sugar	45 mL
½ c.	water	125 mL
20-oz. can	lychees	565-g can
1 t.	lemon juice	5 mL
2 T.	ginger brandy	30 mL
2 T.	Mandarine Napoléon or Grand Marnier liqueur	30 mL
	vanilla ice cream or orange sherbet	

Combine marmalade, sugar, and water in a saucepan or chafing dish. Simmer over low heat about 5 minutes or until syrupy. Drain the lychees, add to the syrup, reserving the juice for another dessert. Continue cooking over low heat only until lychees are hot. Stir in the lemon juice. Remove lychees to a serving dish. Heat brandy and liqueur to a near-boil in a small saucepan; pour over the lychees; ignite. Pour marmalade syrup over flambéed lychees. Serve hot.

CHINESE FRUITS IN GRAND MARNIER

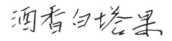

20-oz. can	lychees	565-g can
15-oz. can	loquats	425-g can
3 T.	sugar	45 mL
3 T.	butter	45 mL
2 T.	orange marmalade, warmed	30 mL
⅓ c.	Grand Marnier liqueur	90 mL

Drain lychees and loquats; set aside their juices. In a chafing dish with cover, combine sugar, butter, and marmalade, stirring until sugar dissolves. Cook over very low heat for 4 to 5 minutes. Add lychees and loquats; simmer for 1 minute, basting regularly. Add liqueur; cover for 30 seconds over the same heat. Do *not* flambé. Serve warm in fruit cups.

Note: You can substitute longans or rambutans for the lychees.

FLAMBÉED LYCHEES

耀日荔枝

20-oz. can	lychees	565-g can
4 T.	Grand Marnier or Mandarine Napoléon liqueur	60 mL
1 T.	sugar	15 mL
2 T.	orange marmalade	30 mL

Drain lychees; set aside the juice for another dish. In a saucepan, warm the liqueur; do *not* boil. Gently heat lychees in covered chafing dish or electric skillet; do not cook. Sprinkle lychees with sugar; add the marmalade and stir gently. Add the liqueur; cover for 30 seconds. Stand back, light with a match. When flame goes out, serve in fruit cups.

LYCHEE/RASPBERRY MEDLEY IN CHAMPAGNE

香檳李酒荔莓

20-oz. can	lychees	565-g can
2 c.	plum wine	500 mL
split	iced champagne	split
10-oz. pkg.	frozen raspberries, defrosted	283-g pkg.

Drain lychees; set aside the juice for another dessert. Place lychees in a container with enough wine to cover; refrigerate 1 hour. Drain lychees again, reserving liquid for another dessert. Arrange lychees in a crystal bowl; add 2 c. (500 mL) champagne and ¼ c. (60 mL) chilled, drained raspberries. Serves 7.

Note: To make Longan/Raspberry Medley in Champagne, substitute canned longans for the lychees.

LOQUAT/FROZEN MELON BALLS IN MELON CORDIAL

芳香甜酒瓜球

10-oz. pkg.	frozen melon balls	283-g pkg.
15-oz. can	loquats	425-g can
3 T.	melon liqueur	45 mL

Thaw melon balls; discard the juice. Drain loquats over a bowl; reserve juice for another dessert. Combine melon and loquats in a serving bowl. Pour liqueur over the fruit; cover and refrigerate 1 hour. Serve chilled.

JACKFRUIT IN PLUM WINE

李酒樹波蘿

20-oz. can	jackfruit	565-g can
4 T.	plum wine or Grand Marnier liqueur	60 mL
1 t.	lemon juice	5 mL

Drain the jackfruit; *discard* the jackfruit juice. Rinse the jackfruit thoroughly in tap water. Combine the jackfruit, wine, and lemon juice in a bowl; refrigerate. Serve chilled.

MANDARIN ORANGES & STRAWBERRIES WITH CHINESE LIQUEUR

甜酒草梅柑

11-oz. can	mandarin oranges	311-g can
10-oz. pkg.	frozen strawberries, defrosted	283-g pkg.
¼ c. plus 2 T.	plum wine	90 mL
	nondairy whipped topping (optional)	

Drain oranges; set aside the juice for another dessert. Mix oranges with strawberries. Add the wine and mix. Chill in refrigerator. Serve in fruit cups with topping, if desired.

MANDARIN ORANGES IN WINE & LIQUEUR

甜酒草梅柑

11-oz. can	mandarin oranges	311-g can
1 T.	orange juice	15 mL
2 T.	plum wine	30 mL
1 T.	Mandarine Napoléon or Grand Marnier liqueur	15 mL
2 t.	sugar	10 mL
2	preserved kumquats, pitted and finely chopped	2

Chill oranges in a bowl. Add remaining ingredients and mix well. Refrigerate for 1 hour. Serve in fruit cups.

PLUM WINE & CHINESE LOQUATS

李酒白塔枇杷

15-oz. can	loquats	425-g can
2 T.	butter or margarine	30 mL
½ t.	lemon juice	2 mL
6 T.	granulated brown sugar	90 mL
¼ c.	plum wine	60 mL
	nondairy whipped topping (optional)	

Drain loquats, reserving ⅓ c. (90 mL) of the juice. Melt butter in a large saucepan; stir in the reserved juice. Add lemon juice and brown sugar. Bring to a boil. Add the loquats and simmer for 10 minutes, basting frequently. Stir in the wine; simmer 3 minutes longer. This dessert *must* be served warm. Top with whipped topping, if desired.

Note: You may add 2 T. (30 mL) ginger preserves or orange marmalade after melting the butter.

SWEET PRESERVED PEARS IN PLUM WINE

李酒天津梨

12 pieces	sweet preserved pears (not *anise-flavored*), individually wrapped	12 pieces
1 c.	plum wine (or enough to cover pears in medium bowl)	250 mL
½ T.	sweet white preserved cucumber, very finely chopped	7.5 mL
¼ t.	lemon juice	1 mL

Unwrap the pears and place in a bowl. Mix the wine, cucumber, and lemon juice; pour over the pears. Marinate for 2 hours or, preferably, overnight. Serve in fruit cups.

CHERRIES IN PLUM WINE

李酒櫻桃

17-oz. can	dark sweet cherries (unpitted)	482-g can
2 T.	sugar	30 mL
1 T.	lemon juice	15 mL
½ c.	plum wine	125 mL
2 T.	ginger preserves	30 mL

Drain the cherries and reserve the juice. Place cherries in a bowl. Add ⅛ c. (30 mL) of the cherry juice and remaining ingredients; refrigerate 2 hours. Serve chilled.

GRAPEFRUIT IN PLUM WINE

李酒西柚

2 large	grapefruit, chilled	2 large
2 T.	sugar	30 mL
6 T.	plum wine	90 mL
2 T.	cold orange juice	15 mL

Section the grapefruit; place in a bowl. Add the remaining ingredients. Refrigerate for 1 hour. Serve cold in fruit cups.

Note: To make Pomelo in Plum Wine, substitute 2 large pomelos for the grapefruit.

GINGERED LOQUATS IN PLUM WINE

李酒枇杷

15-oz. can	loquats	425-g can
½ c.	plum wine	125 mL
½ c.	orange juice	125 mL
2 T.	orange marmalade	30 mL
⅛ t.	fresh ginger, grated	.5 mL
3 T.	sugar	45 mL

Drain loquat juice into a small saucepan; set aside the fruit. Add remaining ingredients to the juice. Bring to a boil; lower heat. Add loquats and stir 1 minute; refrigerate. Serve chilled.

PINEAPPLE CHUNKS IN PLUM WINE

李酒波蘿塊

1 small	fresh pineapple or 20-oz. (565-g) can unsweetened pineapple chunks	1 small
6 oz.	plum wine	190 mL
	fresh strawberries or canned lychees, drained	

Cut pineapple into 1-in. (2.5-cm) chunks; if using canned pineapple, drain and set aside juice for another dessert. Add wine to the pineapple in a serving bowl. Marinate in refrigerator for 2 hours. Serve chilled, garnished with strawberries or lychees around the edges of bowl.

Preserves

OUR SPECIAL GINGER PRESERVES

本家薑漿

2 T.	sweet preserved white cucumber	30 mL
1 T.	sweet preserved ginger in syrup	15 mL
2 T.	ginger preserves	30 mL

Finely chop the cucumber and preserved ginger. Mix together all the ingredients. Use as spread or cake topping.

Note: For a very special touch, add 2 t. (10 mL) plum wine.

LYCHEE JAM

荔枝醬

20-oz. can	lychees	565-g can
1 c.	sugar	250 mL
1 T.	lemon juice	15 mL
2 t.	maraschino cherry juice	10 mL
2 oz.	liquid pectin	60 g

Drain the lychees; set aside the juice. Place lychees in blender; blend for 5 seconds until chopped coarsely. In a saucepan mix the lychees, sugar, lemon and cherry juices; mix in ¾ c. (190 mL) of the lychee juice. Bring to a rolling boil over high heat; boil vigorously 15 seconds, stirring constantly; remove from heat; add the pectin. Ladle quickly into jelly jars, cover tightly. Cool for 24 hours in refrigerator. Store in the refrigerator.

Note: For a flavorful variation, stir in 2 t. (10 mL) Grand Marnier liqueur just before ladling jam into the jars.

GINGER/ORANGE MARMALADE PRESERVES

橘皮醬

ginger preserves
orange marmalade

Thoroughly mix equal quantities of ginger preserves with orange marmalade.

Note: To create different combinations for your preserves, substitute peach, red raspberry, black currant, apricot or damson plum preserves for the orange marmalade.

ORANGE/REAL GINGER MARMALADE

8 oz.   orange marmalade   225 g
1 t.   fresh ginger, grated   5 mL

Mix together the marmalade and ginger. Serve in the usual fashion as a uniquely flavored preserve.

Note: By substituting raspberry, strawberry, peach, apricot, black currant, damson plum, or blackberry preserves for the orange marmalade, you can create many different flavors.

ORIENTAL SPIKED MARMALADE OR PRESERVES

For a special treat mixed to your own taste, add a teaspoonful at a time of ginger brandy, Mandarine Napoléon or Grand Marnier liqueur, plum or lychee wine to one of the following: orange, ginger, Dundee triple citrus fruits, or grapefruit marmalade, or peach, damson plum, seedless red raspberry, black currant, or apricot preserves. Keep adding your chosen flavoring until you reach a perfect combination.

LYCHEE PEACHY PRESERVES

3 T.   peach preserves   45 mL
3   lychees, coarsely chopped   3
1 t.   sweet preserved white cucumber, coarsely chopped   5 mL
⅛ t.   lemon juice   .5 mL

Mix all ingredients thoroughly. Use as a spread or topping.

ORIENTAL MARMALADE WITH ORANGE FLAVOR

3 T.   orange marmalade   45 mL
⅛–¼ t.   almond extract   .5–1 mL
1 T.   white sweet preserved cucumber, coarsely   15 mL
              chopped

Mix together all the ingredients. Use as a spread or cake topping.

Note: To make Oriental Marmalade with Orange Flavor & Liqueur, add ¼ to ½ t. (1 to 2 mL) Mandarine Napoléon or Grand Marnier liqueur.

ORIENTAL PRESERVE DELIGHT

4 t.   ginger preserves   20 mL
4 T.   orange marmalade   60 mL
4 T.   preserved kumquats, finely chopped, seeds   60 mL
           removed
¼ t.   lemon juice   1 mL
¼ t.   fresh ginger, grated   1 mL

Mix thoroughly all ingredients. Use as a spread or cake topping.

Note: For an oriental super delight, add ½ t. (2 mL) Mandarine Napoléon or Grand Marnier liqueur.

PLUM WINE JELLY

李酒果醬

3 c.	sugar	750 mL
2 c.	plum wine	500 mL
1½ oz.	container liquid pectin	42.5 mL

Mix the sugar and wine in a saucepan. Stirring constantly, heat until sugar dissolves; remove from heat. Immediately stir in the pectin; refrigerate. Store in covered container in the refrigerator.

Note: If desired, jelly may be stored indefinitely in sterilized and sealed jelly glasses.

LYCHEE/APRICOT PRESERVES

荔杏醬

| 3 T. | apricot preserves | 45 mL |
| 3 | lychees, coarsely chopped | 3 |

Mix preserves and lychees until well blended. Use as a spread.

GINGER MARMALADE WITH LYCHEES

荔枝薑醬

| 3 or more | lychees | 3 or more |
| 1 jar | ginger marmalade | 1 jar |

Blot lychees thoroughly on paper towelling; chop into small pieces. Add lychees to the marmalade, mixing well, adding more lychees to your taste.

Note: To vary the marmalade flavor, instead of the lychees, add 5 chopped longans, 2 chopped rambutans, or 2 T. (30 mL) peach preserves to the marmalade.

GINGER LINGONBERRY PRESERVES

齡今康醬果薑醬

2 T.	ginger preserves	30 mL
2 T.	lingonberries in sugar	30 mL
1 T.	sweet preserved white cucumber, coarsely chopped	15 mL

Mix all the ingredients thoroughly. Use as a spread or topping.

CRUNCHY ORIENTAL APRICOT PRESERVES

薑花杏脯浆

2 T.	apricot preserves	30 mL
2 T.	fresh ginger, grated	30 mL
1 T.	sweet preserved white cucumber, coarsely chopped	15 mL

Mix thoroughly all ingredients. Use as a spread or topping.

Creams, Custards,
Puddings & Mousses

LYCHEE TOFU CUSTARD

荔枝豆腐蛋撻

8-oz.	tofu	225 g
1 c.	lychee juice from 1 can lychees	250 mL
2 t.	sugar	10 mL
1 t.	vanilla	5 mL
1	egg white	1

Beat all ingredients in blender until thick and custardy. Pour into individual custard cups; chill.

Note: To make Mandarine Napoléon Tofu Custard, follow directions above, adding 1 T. (15 mL) Mandarine Napoléon liqueur when blending.

STRAWBERRY TOFU PUDDING

草梅豆腐布甸

10-oz. pkg.	frozen strawberries	283-g pkg.
6 oz.	chilled tofu	180 g
4 T.	corn syrup	60 mL

Mix all ingredients in blender; blend until smooth. Refrigerate for 2 hours; serve in small dessert dishes or use as topping over waffles, pancakes, crepes, and other desserts.

LONGAN/MANDARIN ORANGE TOFU

龍柑豆腐

6 oz.	chilled tofu, cubed	180 g
11-oz. can	mandarin oranges	311-g can
1 T.	corn syrup	15 mL
2 T.	ginger preserves	30 mL
½ 15-oz. can	longans, drained	½ 425-g can
2 t.	Grand Marnier liqueur (optional)	10 mL

Gently mix the first 4 ingredients in a large bowl. Place longans in blender; blend for 20 seconds. Add longans to the tofu mixture, mixing well. Add liqueur, if desired. Chill for 4 hours. Serve in dessert dishes.

MANDARIN ORANGE SOUFFLÉ

甜柑蛋白奶酥

11-oz. can	mandarin oranges	311-g can
2–3 T.	sugar	30–45 mL
4–5	eggs	4–5
¼ c.	sugar	60 mL
3 T.	margarine or butter	45 mL
3 T.	all-purpose flour	45 mL
¼–½ t.	orange peel, grated	1–2 mL
1 T.	Mandarine Napoléon or Grand Marnier liqueur	15 mL

Drain oranges; set aside the juice for another dessert. Process oranges in blender or food processor until smooth; add enough sugar to sweeten. Separate eggs; whip whites until stiff. Gradually add ¼ c. (60 mL) sugar; continue beating until whites form soft peaks. Melt margarine in a saucepan; stir in the flour. Blend oranges into the margarine and flour. Cook until thickened, stirring constantly. Remove from heat, add the yolks, grated orange, and liqueur. Fold half of the whites into the soufflé; then fold in remainder of the whites.

Pour soufflé into buttered and sugar-dusted 1½–qt . (1½–L) soufflé dish, fitted with lightly buttered rim of foil placed around edge of dish to contain the overflow. Bake at 375 °F (190 °C) for 15 minutes. Gently remove foil rim; sprinkle soufflé with sugar. Continue baking for 15 minutes or more. Serve piping hot.

PEANUT MOUSSE

花生鬆糕,

½ lb.	peanut brittle	225 g
2 c.	heavy cream	500 mL
⅓ c.	sugar	90 mL
½ c.	unsalted peanuts, coarsely chopped	125 mL

Coarsely chop peanut brittle in a food chopper. Whip cream with sugar. Quickly add the peanut brittle; spoon into ice tray. Freeze until firm. Serve garnished with peanuts.

FROZEN ALMOND HONEY CREAM

杏仁蜜奶油

3	eggs, separated	3
3 T.	light honey	45 mL
pinch	cream of tartar	pinch
1 c.	heavy cream	250 mL
⅓ c.	almonds, chopped	90 mL
½ t.	almond extract, more to taste	2 mL

Beat egg yolks and honey, using a wire whisk in top of double boiler. Place over simmering water and cook, stirring slowly but steadily with wooden spoon, until slightly thickened, about 8 to 10 minutes; do not boil. Remove from heat and cool; chill. Beat whites until frothy. Add cream of tartar and beat until stiff. Whip heavy cream until it forms soft peaks; add the almonds. Stir almond extract into the chilled yolk mixture. Fold in the whites and whipped cream. Freeze until firm. Makes approximately 1 qt. (1 L).

AGAR-AGAR DELIGHT

東洋菜糕,

¼ c.	brown sugar	60 mL
¾ c.	white sugar	190 mL
3½ c.	water	875 mL
2 sticks	agar-agar	2 sticks

2 t.	vanilla extract	10 mL
1	egg, beaten well	1
½ t.	salt	2 mL
1 c.	coconut juice	250 mL

Combine brown and white sugars; stir in the water. Cook until sugars dissolve. Add agar-agar and vanilla; stir. Mix the egg, salt, and coconut juice; add to agar-agar mixture. Continue cooking until it just simmers. Pour into container and cool; do not move container until mixture has cooled and congealed firmly.

LYCHEE TAPIOCA CREAM

荔枝西米鬆糕

20-oz. can	lychees	565-g can
2	egg yolks, lightly beaten	2
2 c.	milk	500 mL
2 T.	sugar	30 mL
2 T.	quick-cooking tapioca	30 mL
¼ t.	salt	1 mL
1 t.	vanilla extract	5 mL
2	egg whites	2
¼ c.	sugar	60 mL
	light or heavy cream (optional)	

Drain lychees and set aside the juice for another dessert. Coarsely chop the lychees; drain well. Combine the yolks, milk, sugar, tapioca, and salt in a saucepan. Cook over low heat, stirring constantly, until mixture boils; cool, then chill. Stir in the vanilla. Beat whites until foamy. Add sugar, 1 T. (15 mL) at a time, beating until stiff and glossy. Fold tapioca mixture into the whites, then fold in the lychees. Serve in dessert dishes with cream, if desired.

PEACH TOFU CUSTARD

桃子豆腐蛋撻

8 oz.	tofu	225 g
1½ c.	frozen peaches	375 mL
2 t.	sugar	10 mL
¹⁄₁₆ t.	ground cinnamon	.25 mL
½ t.	lemon juice	2 mL
1	egg white	1

Mix all ingredients in blender until thick and custardy. Spoon into custard cups. Chill and serve.

MANDARIN ORANGES WITH TOFU

香甜橘子豆腐

6-oz.	Chinese-style tofu	180 g
11-oz. can	mandarin oranges	311-g can
1 T.	corn syrup	15 mL
2 T.	orange marmalade	30 mL
2 t.	Grand Marnier liqueur	10 mL

Cut tofu into ½-in. (13-mm) cubes. Gently mix tofu with the oranges, syrup, marmalade, and liqueur in a large bowl. Chill 4 hours in refrigerator. Serve in dessert dishes.

Note: To make tofu with Triple Orange Flavor, follow directions above, adding 2 t. (10 mL) Mandarine Napoléon liqueur after refrigerating the dessert.

GINGER LEMON PUDDING CAKE

薑花柠檬布甸糕,

3	eggs, separated	3
2 T.	light molasses	30 mL
6 T.	sugar	90 mL
2 T.	flour	30 mL
1 T.	melted butter	15 mL
2 T.	fresh ginger, grated	30 mL
pinch	salt	pinch
1 c.	milk	250 mL
2 t.	grated lemon peel	10 mL
¼ c.	lemon juice	60 mL

Beat yolks in a mixing bowl. Beat in the remaining ingredients except the whites. In a separate bowl, beat the whites until stiff. Fold whites into the yolk mixture. Pour into square baking pan; set in another pan with hot water about 1 in. (2.5 cm) deep. Bake at 325 °F (165 °C) for 55 minutes or until top is brown. Spoon into serving dishes. Serve warm.

LONGAN TAPIOCA PUDDING

龍眼西米布甸

3 T.	quick-cooking tapioca	45 mL
¼ c.	sugar	60 mL
¼ t.	salt	1 mL
¼ t.	ground cinnamon	1 mL
20-oz. can	longans, drained, chopped, and juice reserved	565-g can
2	eggs, separated	2
6 T.	sugar	90 mL

Mix the first 4 ingredients. Add water to the longan juice to make 2 c. (500 mL); add to the tapioca mixture. Beat yolks; add to the pudding mixture. Cook over boiling water, stirring constantly, until slightly thickened, about 10 minutes. Pour into baking dish. Beat whites until stiff; gradually add 6 T. (90 mL) sugar, beating constantly; decorate edges of pudding with beaten whites. Bake 20 minutes at 325 °F (165 °C). Serve warm or cold.

LOTUS SEEDS & LONGAN PUDDING

蓮龍布甸

½ c.	dried lotus seeds	125 mL
¼ c.	pearl tapioca	60 mL
⅓ c.	dried seedless longans (dragon's eyes)	90 mL
¼ c.	sugar	60 mL

Cover lotus seeds with hot water; soak overnight. Wash, remove skin and little green stem (heart) inside. Separate the longans. Place prepared seeds in a saucepan; cover with 1½ qt. (1½ L) water. Bring to a boil, lower heat and let cook for 1 hour or until seeds are soft (a dash of baking soda will hasten the cooking). Add tapioca. Bring to a boil, lower heat and cook for 35 minutes. Add longans; cook for 30 more minutes; add sugar to your taste.

SWEET RICE WINE/EGG CUSTARD

酒糟蛋撻

1 c.	Sweet Rice Wine	250 mL
4	eggs	4
pinch	salt	pinch

Pour wine into 8-in. (20-cm) pie plate. Beat eggs and add the salt; pour over wine. Bake at 375 °F (190 °C) until eggs are firm.

PINEAPPLE TAPIOCA

½ c.	pearl tapioca	125 mL
15-oz. can	crushed pineapple	425-g can
2–4 T.	sugar, to taste	30–60 mL
12	maraschino cherries, cut into halves	12

Place tapioca in a saucepan, cover with 1 qt. (1 L) water, and bring to a boil. Lower heat and cook until transparent, about 1 hour. Add pineapple and sugar, mixing well; bring back to a boil. Garnish with cherries and serve hot.

SOFT EGG CUSTARD WITH PLUM WINE

12	egg yolks	12
¼ c.	sugar	60 mL
1½ c.	plum wine	375 mL
3 T.	Mandarine Napoléon or Grand Marnier liqueur	45 mL

Beat yolks with sugar until very thick and creamy. Place in top of double boiler over hot water. (Do not allow water to boil during cooking.) Heat to *near* boiling point. Heat wine and liqueur in a saucepan. Slowly add to the custard, beating constantly with rotary beater. Continue to stir while cooking until the custard is thick and hot. Serve hot in sherbet or wine glasses. Serves 6 to 8. Recipe can be halved to serve 3 to 4.

Note: To use the egg whites reserved from this recipe, try Almond Parfait.

GINGER MARMALADE PUDDING/CAKE

2	eggs	2
1 c.	sugar	250 mL
⅔ c.	sifted all-purpose flour	180 mL
¼ t.	salt	1 mL
2½ t.	baking powder	12 mL
4 T.	ginger marmalade preserves	60 mL
1 c.	blanched almonds, chopped (optional)	250 mL
3 t.	lemon juice	15 mL
	whipped cream or nondairy whipped topping (optional)	

Beat eggs thoroughly. Gradually add sugar, beating until fluffy. Sift flour again with salt and baking powder. Sift the flour mixture into the egg mixture, blending well. Mix together the preserves, almonds, and lemon juice; then fold into the egg mixture. Pour into buttered 9-in. (23-cm)-square baking dish. Bake at 350 °F (175 °C) for 30 minutes. Cut into squares. Serve warm or cold, topped with whipped cream, if desired.

LYCHEE FOOL (TRIFLE)

20-oz. can	lychees	565-g can
	red food coloring	
2 c.	heavy cream	500 mL
4 T.	sugar	60 mL

Drain lychees and set aside the juice for another dessert. Finely chop the lychees; add several drops of food coloring. Refrigerate for 1 hour. Beat cream and sugar until stiff. Fold lychees gently into the whipped cream; add food coloring. Serve chilled in sherbet or parfait glasses.

Gels, Whips & Yogurt Desserts

NONA WONG'S PROSPEROUS PUDDING 福祿寿布甸

This colorful dessert represents many symbols of joy: The gold color of the loquats symbolizes wealth; the red color of the gelatin and strawberries symbolizes good fortune and happiness; the green of the kiwi symbolizes growth and long life.

1½ pkg. (4.5 oz.)	ladyfingers	1½ pkg. (135 g)
6-oz. pkg.	strawberry flavored gelatin	180-g pkg.
20-oz. can	pineapple chunks, drained	565-g can
6-oz. pkg.	instant vanilla pudding	180-g pkg.
2 c.	heavy cream, whipped or extra-creamy nondairy whipped topping	500 mL
15-oz. can	loquats, drained, and cut into halves or quarters	425-g can
2 c.	fresh strawberries, cut in half	500 mL
2	kiwi fruit, peeled and sliced crosswise into 8 to 9 pieces	2

Line 3-qt. (3-L) glass bowl with ladyfingers, allowing ¼ in. (6-mm) to extend over top of bowl. Follow package directions to prepare gelatin, substituting the pineapple syrup for part of the cold water specified on the package. When gelatin is softly set add drained pineapple; gently pour into bowl with the ladyfingers. Allow to set. Prepare pudding according to package directions; add to firmly set gelatin. Spread whipped cream over top; refrigerate. Arrange loquats in the middle of the pudding. Arrange strawberries around loquats and kiwi pieces around the strawberries.

PEACHY GINGER YOGURT 桃薑乳酪

8 oz.	peach yogurt	225 g
1½ T.	orange marmalade	22.5 mL
2 T.	ginger preserves	30 mL

Mix thoroughly the yogurt, marmalade, and preserves. Serve chilled.

LYCHEE LEMON ICE WHIP

柠荔鬆夫

20-oz. can	lychees	565-g can
1 t.	unflavored gelatin	5 mL
3 T.	sugar	45 mL
½ t.	vanilla extract	2 mL
1 drop	yellow food coloring	1 drop
½ c.	lemon ice	125 mL

Drain lychees over a bowl. Chop 14 lychees in blender until coarsely puréed. In a saucepan, add gelatin to 1 c. (250 mL) of the juice; warm gently until gelatin dissolves. Add puréed lychees, sugar, vanilla, and coloring. Chill until syrupy. Whip in a chilled bowl until doubled in bulk. Beat in the lemon ice. Refrigerate for 4 hours before serving.

SOYBEAN MILK DESSERT

薑汁豆醬凍

| 5 c. | Soybean Milk | 1250 mL |
| 2 env. | unflavored gelatin | 2 env. |

Pour soybean milk into a saucepan. Sprinkle gelatin in and mix well; dissolve over medium heat. Pour mixture into a bowl; cool. Refrigerate until set. Cut into cubes and serve with Ginger Sugar Syrup.

ALMOND/ORANGE MARMALADE YOGURT

杏仁橘醬乳酪

8 oz.	plain yogurt	225 g
¾ t.	almond extract	4 mL
2½ T.	orange marmalade	37.5 mL
	maraschino cherry (optional)	

Mix all ingredients. Chill 1 hour in refrigerator. Serve in dessert cups, garnished with a cherry.

BOYSENBERRY YOGURT
WITH CHINESE FLAVORS

補生漿果乳酪

8 oz.	boysenberry yogurt	225 g
2 t.	ginger preserves	10 mL
1 T.	sweet white preserved cucumber, coarsely chopped	15 mL

Mix all ingredients. Serve chilled.

MANDARIN ORANGE YOGURT

甜柑乳酪

| 11-oz. can | mandarin oranges | 311-g can |
| 8 oz. | plain yogurt | 225 g |

Drain oranges; set aside the juice for another dessert; purée oranges for 10 seconds in blender. Measure ¼ c. (60 mL) of the purée; fold into the yogurt. Chill before serving.

ALMOND-FLAVORED YOGURT

杏仁乳酪

| 8 oz. | plain yogurt | 225 g |
| ½ t. | almond extract | 2 mL |

Mix thoroughly the yogurt and flavoring. Chill 1 hour in refrigerator before serving.

LYCHEE GELATIN

柠荔凍

20-oz. can	lychees	565-g can
1 T.	unflavored gelatin	15 mL
¼ c.	cold water	60 mL
¾ c.	water	190 mL
2 T.	lemon juice	30 mL
4 T.	sugar	60 mL
1 drop	yellow food coloring	1 drop

Drain lychees and set aside the juice. Cut lychees in quarters. Soften gelatin in ¼ c. (60 mL) cold water. Bring ¾ c. (190 mL) water to a boil in saucepan; dissolve softened gelatin in the boiling water. Add lychee juice and remaining ingredients; cool. When gelatin is about to set, add lychees. Pour setting gelatin mixture into mould or bowl. Chill for 4 hours and serve.

PLUM WINE ELEGANCE

优美李酒

11-oz. can	mandarin oranges	311-g can
3 env.	unflavored gelatin	3 env.
3 c.	water	750 mL
1½ c.	sugar	375 mL
1 c. plus 2 T.	plum wine	250 mL plus 30 mL
3 T.	lemon juice, strained	45 mL
9 drops	red food coloring	9 drops
	nondairy whipped topping (optional)	

Drain oranges and set aside; measure ¼ c. (60 mL) of the juice. Mix the gelatin and water well. Place gelatin mixture in a large saucepan; add the sugar. Stir over medium heat until dissolved. Remove from heat; blend in wine, orange juice, lemon juice, and coloring. Pour mixture into mould or china bowl. Chill until firm. Serve with topping, if desired.

LYCHEE/LONGAN/MANDARIN ORANGE GEL DESSERT

荔龍柑凍点

20-oz. can	lychees	565-g can
15-oz. can	longans	425-g can
11-oz. can	mandarin oranges	311-g can
1 t.	unflavored gelatin	5 mL
¼ t.	almond extract	1 mL

Prepare the fruits as in Lychee/Longan/Mandarin Orange Nectar. For each cup (250 mL) of fruit mixture add 1 t. (5 mL) unflavored gelatin softened in 4 t. (20 mL) water. Mix with the fruits. Add the almond extract. Serve iced or with Lychee Ice Cubes.

LYCHEE RING

荔枝环·

20-oz. can	lychees	565-g can
⅛ c.	lemon juice	30 mL
1 env.	unflavored gelatin	1 env.
2 T.	currant jelly	30 mL
1 c.	cold water	250 mL

Drain lychees and set aside the juice. Mix 1 c. (250 mL) of the juice, the lemon juice, and gelatin in a saucepan. Simmer until gelatin dissolves and pour into a serving bowl. Dissolve the jelly in ⅔ c. (180 mL) cold water and add to the gelatin mixture. Stir in the lychees. Refrigerate until set and ready to serve.

RAINBOW ALMOND FLOAT

虹彩杏仁豆腐

2 env.	unflavored gelatin	2 env.
1 c.	cold water	250 mL
1 c.	evaporated milk	250 mL
1¾ c.	water	440 mL
¼ c.	sugar	60 mL
2 t.	almond extract	10 mL
1–2 drops	green coloring	1–2 drops
1 drop	red coloring	1 drop
20-oz. can	lychees	565-g can
20-oz. can	pineapple chunks	565-g can

Sprinkle gelatin in water; heat over low flame until gelatin dissolves. Add the next 4 ingredients and mix well. Divide mixture into 3 even portions, using loaf pans. Add green coloring to 1 portion, red to the second, leaving the third uncolored. Refrigerate until set. Cut into small cubes and add lychees and pineapple. Refrigerate until serving time.

LONGAN WHIP

15-oz. can	longans	425-g can
1 t.	unflavored gelatin	5 mL
2 t.	lemon juice	10 mL
2 T.	sugar	30 mL
½ t.	vanilla extract	2 mL
1 drop	yellow food coloring	1 drop
½ c.	lemon ice (optional)	125 mL

Drain longans and set aside the juice. Place 28 longans in blender and chop until nearly puréed. In a saucepan, add gelatin to 1 c. (250 mL) of the longan juice. Warm gently over medium heat until dissolved. Add puréed longans, lemon juice, sugar, vanilla, and coloring. Chill until syrupy. Whip mixture in a chilled bowl until doubled in bulk. Beat in the lemon ice, if using. Chill 4 hours before serving.

LYCHEE WHIP

20-oz. can	lychees	565-g can
1 t.	unflavored gelatin	5 mL
3 T.	sugar	45 mL
½ t.	vanilla extract	2 mL
1 drop	yellow food coloring	1 drop
1 t.	lemon juice	5 mL

Drain lychees over a bowl. Chop 14 lychees in blender until coarsely puréed. In a saucepan, add gelatin to 1 c. (250 mL) of the lychee juice; warm gently until dissolved. Add puréed lychees and remaining ingredients. Chill until syrupy. Whip in a chilled bowl until doubled in bulk. Chill for 4 hours before serving.

CHINESE DATE WHIP

2 T.	lemon juice	30 mL
2	egg whites	2
⅛ t.	salt	.5 mL
½ c.	sugar	125 mL
11-oz. can	Chinese date jam	311-g can
	nondairy whipped topping (optional)	

Beat lemon juice and egg whites with salt until frothy. Gradually add sugar, beating until stiff peaks are formed. Fold into jam until blended. Spoon into dessert cups. Chill thoroughly. Serve chilled with topping, if desired.

GINGER YOGURT

1 c.	plain yogurt	250 mL
3 T.	ginger preserves	45 mL
½ t.	maraschino cherry juice	2 mL
3	maraschino cherries	3

Thoroughly mix the yogurt, preserves, and juice. Chill 60 minutes in refrigerator. Serve in dessert cups garnished with the cherries. Serves 2.

LONGAN/STRAWBERRY GELATIN

20-oz. can	longans	565-g can
1 pkg.	strawberry gelatin	1 pkg.
2 t.	lemon juice	10 mL

Drain longans and set aside the juice. Dissolve gelatin in 1 c. (250 mL) boiling longan juice; add the lemon juice. Cool mixture for 10 minutes; add the longans. Chill in refrigerator until set.

Sauces

GINGER SAUCE

1½ c.	ginger jam	375 mL
½ c.	water	125 mL
2 T.	sugar	30 mL
¼ t.	fresh ginger, grated	1 mL

薑醬

Combine all ingredients in a saucepan. Bring to a boil; cook over low heat 5 minutes. Serve hot or cold over lychees, loquats, longans, other sliced fruits, ice cream, or cake.

Note: To make Ginger/Liqueur Sauce follow directions above, adding 2 T. (30 mL) Mandarine Napoléon liqueur, to taste, after cooking the sauce.

DATE JAM TOFU SAUCE

1½ 11-oz. cans	date jam	1½ 311-g cans
8 oz.	tofu	250 mL
1½ T.	lemon juice	22.5 mL

枣蓉豆腐醬

Blend all ingredients until smooth. Chill for 2 hours. Serve in dessert cups.

LINGONBERRY CHINESE SAUCE

1 T.	lingonberries in sugar	15 mL
2 T.	lychee juice	30 mL
1 T.	sweet preserved white cucumber, coarsely chopped	15 mL

齡康果醬

Mix all ingredients. Use as dessert sauce.

FONDUE WARM SAUCE

2 T.	butter or margarine, softened	30 mL
¾ c.	brown sugar, firmly packed	190 mL
¼ t.	salt	1 mL
½ c.	hot evaporated milk	125 mL

奶油热醬

Mix the butter, brown sugar, and salt. Stir into the hot milk until blended.

ALMOND CRÈME SAUCE

杏仁奶油醬

1 c.	heavy cream	250 mL
2 T.	sugar	30 mL
¾ t.	vanilla extract	4 mL
½ t.	lemon extract	2 mL
¾ t.	almond extract	4 mL

Whip the cream and sugar together until stiff. Mix the flavorings and add to the cream. Serve over cake, pudding, ice cream, and other desserts.

Note: To make Ginger Crème Sauce, follow directions above, substituting 2 T. (30 mL) preserved stem ginger, coarsely chopped, or ginger preserves for the almond extract. To prepare Kumquat Crème Sauce, follow directions above, substituting 2 T. (30 mL) preserved kumquats, finely chopped, for the almond extract.

LYCHEE SAUCE

荔枝浆

20-oz. can	lychees	565-g can
1 T.	cornstarch, more if desired	15 mL
2 T.	lemon juice	30 mL
1 T.	grenadine syrup or several drops red food coloring	15 mL
2 T.	Mandarine Napoléon or Grand Marnier liqueur (optional)	30 mL

Drain lychee juice into blender and add 8 lychees; refrigerate the remaining fruit. Blend lychee juice and fruit for 10 seconds only. Pour blender contents into a saucepan; add the cornstarch, lemon juice, and grenadine. Heat to a slow boil, stirring constantly until mixture thickens. If desired, thicken with 1 t. (5 mL) cornstarch mixed with 1 T. (15 mL) cold water. Add liqueur and stir well. Serve sauce over the reserved lychees or over chilled loquats, fresh-cut fruit, seedless grapes, or cake.

HOT CRANBERRY/ MANDARIN ORANGE SAUCE

酸果蔓柑热醬

11-oz. can	mandarin oranges	311-g can
16-oz. can	jellied cranberry sauce	454-g can
½ t.	fresh ginger, shredded, or ginger preserves	2 mL
1 T.	Mandarine Napoléon or Grand Marnier liqueur	15 mL

Drain oranges; set aside juice for another dessert. Chop oranges coarsely in blender. Add remaining ingredients to oranges in blender; process for 20 seconds. Pour into a saucepan; heat, stirring occasionally; simmer 30 seconds. Serve hot or warm. Serve over canned or fresh freestone peaches, apricots, pears, or other fruits.

GINGER HONEY SAUCE

薑蜜醬

½ c.	honey	125 mL
½ c.	ginger brandy	125 mL
2 T.	ginger preserves	30 mL

Mix honey, brandy, and preserves. Spoon over ice cream, sherbet, or cake.

MANDARIN ORANGE DESSERT GEL/SAUCE

橘子甜醬

11-oz. can	mandarin oranges	311-g can
1½ oz.	fruit pectin	45 g
1 c.	water	250 mL
2 c.	sugar	500 mL

Place the fruit and juice in blender; blend thoroughly. In a saucepan stir oranges, pectin, and water until pectin dissolves. Cook over high heat about 2 minutes, stirring constantly, until mixture comes to a rolling boil. Add sugar; heat again to a rolling boil, stirring constantly; remove from heat. Skim off any foam. Refrigerate for 3 hours. Serve as a dessert or sauce.

Note: To make Mandarin Orange/Liqueur Dessert Gel/Sauce, follow directions above, adding 3 T. (45 mL) Mandarine Napoléon liqueur just before serving. To prepare Lychee Dessert Gel/Sauce, follow directions above, substituting half of a 20-oz. (565-g) can lychees (fruit and juice) for the mandarin oranges. To make Longan Dessert Gel/Sauce, follow directions above, substituting half of a 15-oz. (425-g) can longans (fruit and juice) for the mandarin oranges.

GINGER WINE SAUCE

李酒薑醬

1 c.	ginger preserves	250 mL
2 T.	water	30 mL
¼ c.	plum wine	60 mL
½ t.	fresh ginger, grated	2 mL

Stir preserves and water in a small saucepan over moderate heat until mixture comes to a boil; remove from heat. Stir in the wine and ginger. Serve warm or at room temperature. Sauce may be refrigerated and warmed slightly before serving on custards or puddings.

GINGER PRESERVES SAUCE

薑果醬

| ½ c. | ginger preserves | 125 mL |
| 2 T. | water | 30 mL |

Combine preserves and water. Serve with ice cream.

ALMOND SAUCE

杏仁醬

½ c.	margarine	125 mL
⅓ c.	confectioners' sugar	90 mL
1	egg	1
½ t.	almond extract	2 mL

Cream margarine and gradually add the sugar. Beat in the egg and almond extract. Place in the top of a double boiler over hot water. Heat the sauce, beating constantly with an egg beater until fluffy. Serve hot.

LYCHEE-MELBA SAUCE

荔枝梅与巴浆

10-oz. pkg.	frozen strawberries or raspberries	283-g pkg.
20-oz. can	lychees	565-g can
½ c.	currant jelly	125 mL
1 t.	lemon juice	5 mL

Thaw strawberries or raspberries; purée in blender. Drain lychees; set aside the juice for another dessert. Blend lychees coarsely for 5 to 10 seconds (do not purée them). Combine strawberries, jelly, and lemon juice in a saucepan. Heat until jelly completely dissolves. Add the lychees and heat to a simmer, mixing thoroughly. Serve cool or warm over peaches, crepes, longans, loquats, baked apple, applesauce, or spongecake.

LONGAN LIQUEUR SAUCE

龍眼酒醬

20-oz. can	longans	565-g can
¼ c.	sugar	60 mL
1 t.	lemon juice	5 mL
⅛ t.	almond extract (optional)	.5 mL
2 T.	Mandarine Napoléon or Grand Marnier liqueur	30 mL
2 t.	cornstarch	10 mL
4 T.	water	60 mL

Drain longan juice into a small saucepan; reserve the fruit. Add the next 4 ingredients. Heat, stirring constantly, until sauce thickens. Dissolve cornstarch in water; add to the sauce. Stir in half the reserved longans. Serve over dessert, cakes, or as filling for omelette.

LYCHEE/LEMON SAUCE

柠檬荔枝醬

20-oz. can	lychees	565-g can
1 c.	sugar	250 mL
½ c.	butter or margarine, at room temperature	125 mL
2 T.	lemon juice, to taste	30 mL
1	egg	1

Drain lychees over a bowl and set aside the fruit. Combine the sugar, butter and lemon juice in a saucepan. Slowly heat, stirring constantly, until butter and sugar blend. In a bowl, beat the egg with ½ c. (125 mL) of the lychee juice. Gradually beat ¼ c. (60 mL) of the hot sauce into the beaten egg; repeat. Stir mixture into the sauce in the saucepan. Cook for 1 minute until the sauce thickens. This sauce *must* be served hot or warm. Serve over lychees, ice cream, or cakes.

ORANGE SAUCE

橘子醬

½ jar	orange marmalade	½ jar
1 c.	water	250 mL
2 T.	Mandarine Napoléon liqueur	30 mL

Mix marmalade and water in a saucepan; heat slowly just to a boil; simmer for 7 or 8 minutes. Stir in the liqueur. Serve over custard, pudding, cake, ice cream, or slightly warm over chilled strawberries, orange segments or other fruits.

PEANUT BUTTER SAUCE

奶油花生浆

1 c.	sugar	250 mL
1 T.	light corn syrup	15 mL
¾ c.	milk	190 mL
⅛ t.	salt	.5 mL
2 T.	butter	30 mL
⅓ c.	smooth peanut butter	90 mL
½ t.	vanilla extract	2 mL

Mix sugar, syrup, milk and salt in a 2 qt. (2 L) saucepan. Stir over moderate heat and bring to a boil. Insert a candy thermometer; lower heat so that sauce boils gently, without stirring, for 30 to 40 minutes or until thermometer registers 225 to 228 °F (107 to 190 °C) and sauce thickens and turns light golden brown. Remove from heat; add butter and peanut butter; stir briskly with small wire whisk until smooth; then add the vanilla. Serve sauce warm (keeping warm or reheated in small double boiler over hot water on moderate heat, stirring occasionally). When served over ice cream, sauce thickens to a hard caramel consistency.

WARM PLUM WINE PUDDING SAUCE

李酒布甸热浆

½ c.	butter	125 mL
1 c.	sugar	250 mL
2	eggs	2
½ c.	plum wine or 2 T. (30 mL)	125 mL
	Mandarine Napoléon	
	liqueur or ginger brandy	
1 t.	lemon rind, grated	5 mL

Cream butter and sugar. Beat eggs until frothy and add the butter and sugar, mixing well. Add the wine or liqueur and grated rind. Heat thoroughly until almost boiling in top of a double boiler—until just *before* the eggs cook to make a thick sauce.

Note: To make Warm Mandarine Napoléon Liqueur Pudding Sauce, substitute 2 T. (30 mL) Mandarine Napoléon liqueur for the plum wine. Use 1½ t. (7 mL) grated rind. Add 1 T. (15 mL) ginger preserves to the sauce before heating.

PLUM WINE SYRUP

李酒糖汁

¼ c.	sugar	60 mL
½ c.	water	125 mL
6 T.	plum wine	90 mL
1 T.	water chestnut powder or 1 t. (5 mL) cornstarch	15 mL
1 T.	water	15 mL

Combine sugar and water in a saucepan; bring to a boil and add the wine. Mix the water chestnut powder or cornstarch with the water. While the syrup is barely simmering, add the cornstarch mixture slowly until the syrup is desired thickness. Serve over cake, fruit, or ice cream.

RAMBUTAN IN MARASCHINO CHERRY SAUCE

20-oz. can	rambutans	565-g can
⅜ c.	sugar	90 mL
1 T.	water chestnut powder or 1 t. (5 mL) cornstarch	15 mL
⅛ c.	light corn syrup	30 mL
⅛ c.	strained orange juice	30 mL
⅛ c.	maraschino cherry juice	30 mL
1 drop	red food color (optional)	1 drop
1 t.	water chestnut powder	5 mL
1 T.	water	15 mL

Drain rambutans and set aside the juice. Mix sugar with water chestnut powder in a saucepan; stir in the corn syrup, orange juice, ½ c. (125 mL) of the rambutan juice, cherry juice, and coloring. Bring to a boil and cook about 3 minutes until the sauce is clear and slightly syrupy. In a cup, mix 1 t. (5 mL) water chestnut powder and the water. Thicken the sauce by adding one third at a time, stirring constantly until the sauce is the desired thickness; remove from heat. Pour sauce over the rambutans. Refrigerate in a covered container for 2 hours before serving.

Note: Lychees, loquats, or longans may be substituted for the rambutans. If you like, add 2 t. (10 mL) Mandarine Napoléon or Grand Marnier liqueur when making the sauce.

Spreads & Toppings

GINGER BUTTER SPREAD

白塔薑醬

| ½ c. | butter | 125 mL |
| ½ c. | ginger preserves | 125 mL |

Beat butter until fluffy; beat in the preserves. Serve as spread over toast and English muffins.

Note: To make Date Jam Butter Spread, follow directions above, substituting ½ c. (125 mL) date jam for the butter. To prepare Kumquat Butter Spread, follow directions for Ginger Butter Spread, substituting ½ c. (125 mL) pitted, minced preserved kumquats for the ginger preserves.

GINGER SWEET RED BEAN DESSERT/SPREAD

薑酒豆沙

½ c.	sweet bean paste	125 mL
2 T.	ginger preserves	30 mL
1 T.	ginger brandy	15 mL
	nondairy whipped topping	

Mix all ingredients well. Serve topped with whipped topping or serve as spread on cake.

Note: You may add 2 t. (10 mL) almond extract with the other ingredients.

FROZEN LYCHEE FLUFF

荔枝奶油鬆糕

20-oz. can	lychees	565-g can
1¼ c.	crisp cookie crumbs	310 mL
⅓ c.	butter	90 mL
2	egg whites	2
1 T.	lemon juice	15 mL
½ c.	sugar	125 mL
1 c.	heavy cream	250 mL

Drain lychees and set aside the juice. Mix cookie crumbs and butter; press on bottom of 7-in. (17-cm)-round springform pan. Bake at 350 °F (175 °C) for 8 minutes; cool. Lightly beat the egg whites with lemon juice in a large bowl. Gradually beat in the lychees and sugar; then beat at high speed for 15 minutes until fluffy. Whip the cream and fold into the whites. Spread mixture over the baked crust. Freeze overnight. Before serving, cut into pie shapes.

PEANUT CREAM TOPPING

花生棉糖浆

¼ c.	creamy-style peanut butter	60 mL
¼ c.	milk	60 mL
¼ c.	marshmallow cream	60 mL

Blend peanut butter with milk; stir in the marshmallow. Serve as topping.

ALMOND TOPPING

杏仁奶油

½ c.	nondairy whipped topping or whipped cream	125 mL
1 T.	sugar	15 mL
½ t.	almond extract	2 mL
1 T.	syrup from loquats, lychees, peaches, or apricots	15 mL

Combine all ingredients in a small bowl. Mix well until creamy; chill. Serve as spread or topping over cake.

ALMOND LYCHEE GLAZE

杏荔浆

10	canned lychees, drained	10
½ c.	corn syrup	125 mL
½ t.	almond extract	2 mL

Purée lychees in blender for 10 seconds; remove to saucepan. Add corn syrup. Heat to the boiling point; reduce heat and simmer for 5 minutes. Remove from heat. Stir in the extract; cool. Serve over spongecake, poundcake or shortcake.

DATE JAM TOPPING

枣蓉凝冻

| 1 c. | cream | 250 mL |
| 4 T. | date jam | 60 mL |

Whip cream until stiff. Fold in the jam, blending well.

MARSHMALLOW GINGER TOPPING

棉糖薑醬

| 2 T. | marshmallow cream | 30 mL |
| 2 T. | ginger preserves | 30 mL |

Mix well the marshmallow topping and preserves.

Note: To make Fluffy Ginger Preserve Topping with Ginger Brandy, add ¼ t. (1 mL) ginger brandy to above recipe. You may substitute ⅛ t. (.5 mL) fresh ginger, grated, for the ginger preserves, if you prefer.

ORANGE TOFU ICING

豆腐橘浆

12 oz.	tofu	360 g
2 T.	corn syrup	30 mL
pinch	salt	pinch
6 T.	orange marmalade	90 mL

Place tofu in middle of a large, dry dish towel; hold corners together and twist until tightly closed; squeeze tofu firmly for 1 minute to release water. Combine tofu and remaining ingredients in blender; blend for 30 seconds. Refrigerate until ready to serve as icing on cake.

Note: To make Ginger Tofu Icing, follow directions for above, substituting 6 T. (90 mL) ginger preserves for the orange marmalade. To prepare Kumquat Tofu Icing, substitute 8 pitted preserved kumquats, freshly chopped, for the orange marmalade.

TWO GINGER TOPPING

双薑凝凍

4 T.	nondairy whipped topping	60 mL
1 T.	ginger preserves	15 mL
⅛ t.	fresh ginger, grated	.5 mL

Gently mix the topping and preserves. Add the ginger, mixing well. Serve as spread over poundcake, spongecake, and other cakes.

MARSHMALLOW TOPPING WITH LIQUEUR

酒香棉糖浆

| 2 T. | marshmallow cream | 30 mL |
| ¼ t. | Mandarine Napoléon or Grand Marnier liqueur | 1 mL |

Mix marshmallow and liqueur.

MARSHMALLOW TOPPING WITH KUMQUATS

金橘棉糖浆

2 T.	marshmallow cream	30 mL
1 T.	preserved kumquat juice	15 mL
1 T.	preserved kumquat, chopped	15 mL

Mix well all the ingredients.

GINGER TOPPING

薑醬奶油

2 t.	ginger preserves	10 mL
1 c.	heavy cream	250 mL
¼ c.	confectioners' sugar	60 mL
1 t. (scant)	vanilla extract	5 mL (scant)
	pecans or walnuts, chopped, or semisweet chocolate, coarsely grated (optional)	

Stir preserves until soft. Spread over cake. In a chilled bowl with chilled beaters, whip cream, sugar, and vanilla until firm. Spread over preserves on the cake. Sprinkle nuts as a final topping.

HONEY/GINGER
MANDARINE NAPOLÉON TOPPING

蜜薑橘酒奶油

2 c.	chilled heavy cream	500 mL
¼ c.	honey	60 mL
4 T.	ginger preserves	60 mL
4 t.	Mandarine Napoléon or Grand Marnier liqueur	20 mL

In a chilled bowl, beat the cream until stiff. Add the honey, preserves, and liqueur, mixing well after each addition. Chill and serve as a spread on cake, over fruit, cookies, and other desserts.

KUMQUAT LIQUEUR TOPPING

金橘酒浆

1½ c.	preserved kumquats	375 mL
½ c.	water	125 mL
3 T.	ginger brandy or Mandarine Napoléon or Grand Marnier liqueur	45 mL

Pit kumquats; purée coarsely in blender, or chop finely by hand. Combine kumquats and remaining ingredients in a small saucepan. Bring to a low boil; simmer over low heat for 7 minutes. Serve hot or cold over ice cream, custard, cake, and other desserts.

GINGER CREAM TOPPING

甜酒糖薑奶油

1 c.	heavy cream	250 mL
2 T.	confectioners' sugar	30 mL
½ t.	vanilla extract	2 mL
2 T.	Mandarine Napoléon or Grand Marnier liqueur	30 mL
2 T.	crystallized ginger, finely cut, or preserved ginger, drained and finely chopped	30 mL

Chill mixing bowl and beaters in the freezer. Mix cream, sugar, vanilla, and liqueur in the chilled bowl. Beat until mixture holds a soft shape. Fold in the ginger; mix well.

GINGER CREAM CHEESE TOPPING

糖薑芝士奶油

3-oz. pkg.	cream cheese, at room temperature	85-g pkg.
½ c.	margarine or butter	125 mL
1 t.	vanilla extract	5 mL
2 c.	sifted confectioners' sugar	500 mL
1–2 drops	green or red food coloring	1–2 drops
½ c.	crystallized ginger, chopped	125 mL

Beat all ingredients thoroughly. Spread on desired cake.

GINGER WHIPPED TOPPING

輕鬆薑漿奶油

| 1 c. | heavy cream | 250 mL |
| 4 T. | ginger preserves | 60 mL |

Whip cream until stiff. Mix preserves until soft and fold into the cream, mixing well.

GINGER SUGAR SYRUP

薑糖汁

1 piece	ginger (size of a walnut)	1 piece
4 pieces	Chinese brown sugar	4 pieces
1 c.	water	250 mL

Crush ginger with side of cleaver. Combine all ingredients in a saucepan, cooking until sugar melts and syrup thickens. Store in tightly covered jar.

LYCHEE MARSHMALLOW FROSTING

酒香荔棉糖霜

20-oz. can	lychees	565-g can
2	egg whites	2
¾ c.	sugar	190 mL
2 T.	Mandarine Napoléon liqueur, to taste	30 mL
¼ t.	cream of tartar	1 mL
1 T.	light corn syrup	15 mL
¾ c.	marshmallow cream or ¼ lb. (120 g) marshmallows, quartered	190 mL

Place lychees with their juice in blender; purée for 10 seconds. Beat egg whites and slowly add the sugar, beating until stiff. Add the liqueur and stir well. Pour the lychee purée into a saucepan. Heat over low flame; simmer for 2 minutes. Fold in the egg white mixture. Add the cream of tartar, corn syrup, and marshmallow; heat until dissolved. Serve as hot or cold spread on cake.

LYCHEE GLAZE/SAUCE

光滑荔枝浆

6 T.	lychee juice, reserved from drained can of lychees	90 mL
6 T.	light corn syrup	90 mL
½ t.	lemon juice	2 mL

Heat lychee juice and corn syrup to a rolling boil. Cool until lukewarm; add the lemon juice. Spread over cake.

Note: To make Longan Glaze/Sauce, use longan juice instead of the lychee juice. You may use loquat juice to make Loquat Glaze instead of the lychee juice.

MANDARINE NAPOLÉON LIQUEUR/ LYCHEE GLAZE

甜酒荔枝浆

6 T.	lychee juice, reserved from drained can of lychees	90 mL
6 T.	light corn syrup	90 mL
½ t.	lemon juice	2 mL
1 t.	Mandarine Napoléon or Grand Marnier liqueur	5 mL

Heat lychee juice and corn syrup to a rolling boil. Cool until lukewarm; add the flavorings. Spread over cake.

PLUM WINE/LONGAN GLAZE/SAUCE

李酒龍汁糖醬

2 t.	plum wine	10 mL
6 T.	longan juice, reserved from drained can of longans	90 mL
6 T.	light corn syrup	90 mL
½ t.	lemon juice	2 mL

Heat wine, longan juice, and corn syrup to a rolling boil. Cool until lukewarm; add the lemon juice. Spread over cake.

KUMQUAT SPREAD/FROSTING

金橘醬

3	preserved kumquats	3
4 T.	nondairy whipped topping	60 mL
2 t.	preserved kumquat syrup	10 mL

Slice the kumquats thinly and discard pits; finely chop the kumquats. Add to the topping; mix gently but well; stir in the syrup (mixture will no longer be light and creamy but have consistency of a spread). Serve as a spread over poundcake or spongecake.

SWEET RED BEAN DESSERT SAUCE

橘浆红豆沙

½ c.	sweetened red bean paste	125 mL
2 T.	orange marmalade	30 mL
1 T.	Mandarine Napoléon or Grand Marnier liqueur	15 mL
	nondairy whipped topping	

Mix the bean paste and marmalade. Stir in the liqueur. Serve chilled with whipped topping or as topping for cake or fruit.

Note: This recipe also makes a flavorful dessert without the marmalade and liqueur.

DIM SUM & SNACKS

Festival & Everyday Dishes

NEW YEAR DUMPLINGS
WITH SWEET BLACK BEAN PASTE

豆沙湯丸

New Year dumplings can be made without any filling, or filled with sweet black bean paste or chunky peanut butter mixed with toasted sesame seeds and brown sugar.

2 c.	glutinous (sweet) rice flour	500 mL
1 c.	cold water	250 mL
½ c.	sweet black bean paste (dow sa)	125 mL
	brown sugar	

Combine flour and water; mix into a smooth dough. Divide into about 30 balls, each 1 in. (2.5 cm) in diameter. Flatten each ball into a 2-in. (5 cm) circle with your hand. Place about 1 t. (5 mL) bean paste in middle of circle; fold dough over, seal edges, and roll again into balls. To cook, boil 6 c. (1½ L) water in a saucepan; add dumplings and stir to prevent sticking. When dumplings float, simmer 5 to 7 minutes longer. For each serving, place 4 to 6 dumplings in a bowl; cover with hot water and add brown sugar to taste.

NEW YEAR DUMPLINGS WITH SWEET RICE WINE

酒釀湯丸

Add about 2 T. (30 mL) Sweet Rice Wine to boiling water for each serving.

NEW YEAR DUMPLINGS WITH PEANUT BUTTER

花生湯丸

⅓ c.	chunky-style peanut butter	90 mL
3 T.	brown sugar	45 mL
1 T.	sesame seeds (optional)	15 mL

Follow directions above, substituting peanut butter, brown sugar, and sesame seeds for the sweet black bean paste.

SPRING ROLL OR EGG ROLL

春捲

In Cantonese, "spring" and "egg" have the same sound and are used interchangeably. Because spring comes shortly after the Chinese New Year, spring rolls are served to guests at the New Year as a way of welcoming the spring and receiving blessings.

1	boneless chicken breast	1
1-oz. pkg.	cellophane noodles	30-g pkg.
¼ c.	cloud ears (optional)	60 mL
2	carrots	2
1–2 stalks	scallion	1–2 stalks
4 oz.	frozen shrimp, minced	120 g
½ lb.	bean sprouts	225 g
1	egg	1
1–2 t.	salt, to taste	5–10 mL
½ t.	black pepper	2 mL
15 wrappers	Shanghai egg roll wrappers	15 wrappers
	vegetable oil for deep frying	

Cut chicken into thin slices and mince. Soak noodles in hot water for half an hour or until soft. Cut into 1-in. (2.5 cm) segments. Soak cloud ears in hot water until soft; wash thoroughly, then chop. Scrape carrots; cut into thin slices, shred or grate. Chop scallion. Combine all the above ingredients, mixing well. Place 2 to 3 T. (30 to 45 mL) of the mixture, shaped in a mound, in middle of each wrapper. To form a roll: Starting with closest corner, fold wrapper over filling; tuck ends towards middle. Juice from filling will seal edges. With sealed edge of roll down deep-fry in oil heated to 375 °F (190 °C) until golden brown, about 3 to 5 minutes. To prevent its opening, use chopsticks or tongs to hold sealed edge, when first placed in oil; release when fried skin stiffens. Turn roll in oil to fry evenly. Makes 15.

COCONUT GLUTINOUS RICE BALLS

椰絲糯米糍

2 c.	glutinous (sweet) rice flour	500 mL
3 T.	sugar	45 mL
1 T.	margarine or lard, melted	15 mL
¼ c.	wheat starch	60 mL
½ c.	boiling water	125 mL
1 c.	bean paste (dow sa)	250 mL
½–¾ c.	coconut flakes	125–190 mL
	green or red cherries	

Place rice flour in a bowl; make a well in middle and add the sugar and margarine. Place starch in another bowl; add boiling water, mixing well with chopsticks. When the starch thickens, add to the rice flour mixture. Mix well and knead; gradually add about ¼ c. (60 mL) cold water to the dough; continue kneading until it is soft and smooth. Divide into 12 to 15 pieces.

Roll each piece into a ball, then flatten with your palms. Place 1 T. (15 mL) bean paste in middle; pinch and seal edge together; roll into a ball. Arrange balls on greased steamer or on a foil pie plate with small holes in bottom. Steam over boiling water for 10 to 12 minutes. Remove balls, roll in coconut until well coated. Garnish top with cherries, if desired.

GLUTINOUS RICE BALLS WITH PEANUT BUTTER

花生糯米糍

Repeat the same procedure to make Coconut Glutinous Rice Balls and substitute the following stuffing: 4–6 T. (60–75 mL) brown sugar, ¾ c. (190 mL) peanut butter, and 2 T. (30 mL) chopped nuts. Stuff according to the above directions, then roll in cornstarch, confectioners' sugar, or coconut flakes.

AUNT DOT'S NIEN GAO (Rice Cake)

炒年糕

½ lb.	pork, shredded	225 g
2 t.	soy sauce	10 mL
1 t.	cornstarch	5 mL
¼ t.	sugar	1 mL
1 t.	vegetable oil	5 mL
6	Chinese dried mushrooms	6
1 c.	chicken broth	250 mL
4 T.	vegetable oil	60 mL
3 slices	fresh ginger, shredded	3 slices
1 clove	garlic, chopped	1 clove
1-2 stalks	scallion, cut into ½-in. (13-mm)-long segments	1-2 stalks
4 c.	green cabbage, cut in bite-sized pieces	1 L
1	carrot, sliced into thin pieces	1
20	snow peas	20
1 lb.	rice cake	450 g
½-1 t.	salt	2-5 mL
	black pepper, to taste	

Mix the pork, soy sauce, cornstarch, sugar, and 1 t. (5 mL) of the oil; marinate for 15 minutes. Rinse the mushrooms and soak in warm water until soft; cut each into 4 to 6 pieces. Add mushroom water to chicken broth to make 1½ c. (375 mL). Heat 4 T. (60 mL) oil in a wok; add ginger, garlic, and scallion. Stir-fry for a few seconds; then add the soaked mushrooms, stirring steadily. Add the marinated pork; stir-fry for 2 to 3 minutes; remove to a dish. Pour excess marinade from pork into the wok; add the cabbage and carrot, mixing well. Stir in 1 c. (250 mL) of the broth and cook until tender, about 3 minutes. Add the snow peas; stir-fry for 2 minutes. Stir in the remaining broth, the rice cake, and scallion, mixing until the rice cake is soft, about 3 minutes. Season with salt and pepper. Serve warm.

STUFFED GLUTINOUS RICE

咸角

1 stalk	scallion	1 stalk
12	Chinese dried black mushrooms	12
20	dried shrimps	20
2 c.	glutinous (sweet) rice flour	500 mL
⅔ c.	hot water	180 mL
3 T.	vegetable oil	45 mL
1 t.	fresh ginger, chopped	5 mL
½ c.	ground pork	125 mL
1 c.	Chinese celery cabbage, chopped	250 mL
½ t.	sugar	2 mL
1 t.	salt	5 mL
dash	MSG (monosodium glutamate) (optional)	dash
	vegetable oil for deep frying	

Remove and discard roots, wash, and chop the scallion. Rinse mushrooms, cover with warm water for 30 minutes or until soft; chop mushrooms. Rinse shrimps; cover with warm water for half an hour; drain and chop. Mix rice flour and water thoroughly. Divide into 18 balls; flatten each ball as thinly as possible with hand. Heat oil. Add scallion, mushrooms, and shrimps; stir-fry for a few seconds. Add ginger and pork; stir-fry for 2 minutes. Add the celery cabbage; stir-fry for 2 more minutes. Add the seasonings, mixing well. Remove filling to a dish and allow it to cool. Fill each patty with 1 T. (15 mL) meat mixture. Fold over, shape each into a half-moon; press along edge to seal. Deep-fry in hot oil until golden brown. Makes 18.

SWEET OLIVE NEW YEAR CAKE

桂花年糕

1 lb.	glutinous (sweet) rice flour	450 g
2 c.	water	500 mL
1½–2 c.	sugar, to taste	375–500 mL
1 t.	sweet olive or vanilla extract	5 mL
1–2 drops	red food coloring (optional)	1–2 drops

Mix all ingredients, blending well. Spread in 7 × 7 × 2-in. (17 × 17 × 5-cm) pan. Steam over boiling water with heat high for 10 minutes. Then lower to medium heat and steam another 50 minutes. Remove from heat and cool. This cake can be kept in refrigerator for weeks or in freezer for months.

To serve, slice in ½ × 2½-in. (1.3 × 6.4-cm) slices; dip in slightly beaten egg; brown both sides until soft in a little oil in a skillet. This cake is good for breakfast or as a snack.

Note: Sweet olive flavor (*kwei hwa jing*) can be purchased in Chinese grocery stores.

WHITE SWEET STEAMED CAKE (Patong Gow)

白糖糕

1 c.	long-grain rice	250 mL
1¼–1½ c.	sugar, to taste	310–375 mL
1 pkg.	active dry yeast	1 pkg.
⅛ t.	boric acid powder	.5 mL

Rinse rice, cover with 2 c. (500 mL) water; let stand for at least 2 days; drain. In a bowl, mix ¼ c. (60 mL) sugar and ½ c. (125 mL) lukewarm water. Sprinkle in the yeast, stir well and let stand. Place ½ c. (125 mL) soaked rice and 1½ c. (375 mL) water in blender; blend at high speed until mixture is liquefied and smooth, about 4 minutes. Pour mixture into a large bowl. Repeat procedure until all rice has been processed. Pour rice mixture back into blender, add remaining sugar and boric acid powder; blend 1½ minutes at high speed. Add yeast mixture; blend at low speed for 30 seconds. Pour mixture into a bowl; let stand in warm oven (heated to 90 °F [32 °C] and turned off) in a pan of hot water until mixture is spongy and doubled, about 2 hours. Stir lightly and pour into a round cake pan, steam over boiling water for 30 minutes. Serve hot or cold.

Note: Cake can be kept in refrigerator for several days or in freezer indefinitely. Resteam for 5 to 10 minutes before serving.

TURNIP CAKE

蔓苔糕

12–15	dried shrimps	12–15
6	Chinese dried mushrooms	6
1 lb.	white turnips	450 g
1½ c.	chicken broth	375 mL
⅓ c.	cornstarch	90 mL
½ c.	mushroom water	125 mL
⅓ c.	Virginia ham, chopped	90 mL
1	Chinese sausage, chopped	1
1½ c.	rice flour	375 mL
½ t.	salt, to taste	2 mL
1–2 T.	Chinese parsley, chopped	15–30 mL

Rinse the shrimps and mushrooms; cover each with warm water for 15 to 30 minutes or until soft; drain and save the mushroom water. Chop finely. Peel and shred the turnips. Cook turnips in the chicken broth for 10 minutes or until soft. Mix the cornstarch and mushroom water. Slowly add to the turnips, mixing well. Add the shrimps, ham, sausage, and mushrooms and bring to a boil. Slowly stir in the rice flour and salt. Pour mixture into a greased pan. Sprinkle with parsley and steam over boiling water for 1 hour; cool. Store in refrigerator. To serve, brown the cake on both sides in a well-greased frying pan. Serve with oyster sauce as a dip, if desired.

NEW YEAR CAKE

年糕，

1 lb.	glutinous (sweet) rice flour	450 g
1½ c.	brown sugar	375 mL
1¼ c.	water	310 mL
¼ c.	lard, melted	60 mL
1 t.	rose or vanilla extract	5 mL
1–3 drops	red food coloring	1–3 drops

Combine all ingredients; beat with beater, mixing well. Grease 3 5-in. (12.7-cm) heatproof bowls; pour batter in. Steam over boiling water for 1 hour.

NINE LAYERED CAKE

九層糕，

2⅔ c.	sugar	680 mL
1 c.	water	250 mL
3½ c.	tapioca flour	875 mL
2 c.	rice flour	500 mL
4 c.	coconut milk	1 L
	red and green food coloring	

Combine the sugar and water, mixing thoroughly. Add the tapioca, rice flour and coconut milk, then divide batter into 2 portions. Divide 1 portion into half. Add green to half and red to the other. The uncolored batter will make the white layer.

To cook, pour 1 to 2 ladles of white batter into a round cake pan and steam over boiling water for 3 minutes. Add another layer of batter (different color) to first layer and steam for 3 minutes. Alternate layers until batter is all used up to make 9 layers and steam the last layer for 15 minutes. Cake may be resteamed before serving.

HAPPY FACE BALLS

閉口枣

2 c.	all-purpose flour	500 mL
¾ c.	sugar	190 mL
1 t.	baking powder	5 mL
½ t.	baking soda	2 mL
⅛ t.	ammonium bicarbonate	.5 mL
1 T.	vegetable oil	15 mL
½ c.	water	125 mL
	sesame seeds to coat balls	
2–3 c.	vegetable oil for deep frying	500–750 mL

Sift together once the first 5 ingredients. Add 2 T. (30 mL) vegetable oil and the water, mixing well. Shape dough into balls, 1 in. (2.5 cm) in diameter. Wet sesame seeds with water; roll each ball in the seeds until coated; let stand for 10 to 15 minutes.

Heat the oil. Fry a few balls at a time, first in hot oil then lower heat and continue to fry until golden brown about 5 minutes. (Cracks appearing in balls will look like happy faces.) Refrigerate or freeze until ready to serve. Makes 18.

BEAN PASTE SESAME BALLS

煎, 堆

½ c.	brown sugar, well packed	125 mL
⅔ c.	boiling water	180 mL
½ lb.	glutinous (sweet) rice flour	225 g
	sweet black bean paste	
	sesame seeds	
	vegetable oil for deep frying	

Melt the brown sugar in boiling water; mix well with rice flour. Shape into small balls; stuff each ball with 1 t. (5 mL) bean paste. Wet sesame seeds with water and roll balls in the seeds. Deep-fry in hot oil until golden brown. Makes 12 balls.

FRIED BANANAS

炸香蕉

4	bananas or 2 plantains	4
⅓ c.	all-purpose flour	90 mL
3 T.	cornstarch	45 mL
½ t.	baking powder	2 mL
½–1 t.	salt	2–5 mL
½ t.	sugar	2 mL
⅓ c.	water	90 mL
2 c.	peanut oil	500 mL

Peel the bananas; slice diagonally into ¾-in. (19-mm)-thick pieces. To make a batter combine remaining ingredients except oil, mixing well. Dip bananas in the batter. Fry a few pieces at a time in heated oil until golden brown. Drain on paper towel. Serve hot or cold.

CANDIED POMELO OR GRAPEFRUIT PEEL

柚皮糖

1	pomelo or 2 Florida grapefruit	1
1 c.	sugar, more for rolling the peels	250 mL
1 c.	water	250 mL
½ c.	light corn syrup	125 mL

Remove skin of the pomelo or grapefruit and cut into 6 strips. Drop the strips into boiling water; cook 8 minutes, then drain. Repeat this process 3 times. Cut into ¼-in. (6-mm) strips. Mix the sugar, water, and corn syrup. Bring to a boil, stirring, over medium heat. Add the strips; mix well. When syrup boils again, lower heat and boil gently until the syrup is completely absorbed, about 35 to 40 minutes; drain. Roll peels in sugar; lay strips individually on a rack and dry for 2 days. Store in a covered jar.

HONEY SPICED PECANS

蜜香山核桃

1	egg white	1
1 t.	water	5 mL
½ lb.	pecan or walnut halves	225 g
1 T.	honey	15 mL
2 T.	sugar	30 mL
¼ t.	five spices powder	1 mL
¼ t.	salt	1 mL

Beat egg white and water until frothy; pour over the nuts and mix well. Add the remaining ingredients to the nuts, stirring well. Spread on buttered cookie sheet; bake at 250 °F (120 °C) for 30 minutes. Turn nuts and bake for 15 more minutes; turn once more and bake for 15 more minutes. When cool, store in airtight can or jar.

BAO TZU DOUGH (Chinese Bread Dough)

¾ c.	warm water	190 mL
1 T.	sugar	15 mL
2 pkg.	active dry yeast	2 pkg.
1¼ c.	skim milk	310 mL
½ c.	sugar	125 mL
1 t.	salt	5 mL
½ c.	vegetable oil	125 mL
2 lb.-box	cake flour	900 g
¾ c.	self-rising cake flour, preferably, for the rolling board	190 mL

In a large bowl, combine the warm water and 1 T. (15 mL) sugar; stir until sugar dissolves. Sprinkle in the yeast and stir well; let stand for 10 minutes, until spongy. Combine milk, ½ c. (125 mL) sugar, and salt in a saucepan; stir well and warm to 90 °F (32.2 °C). Add the oil, mix well and pour into the yeast mixture; mix well. Add the cake flour; stir well with chopsticks or fork; then knead on a board floured with the self-rising flour until dough is elastic and smooth. Form into a ball; pat on a little oil with hands and cover with a wet cloth. Place dough away from a draft or set in unlit oven with a pan of hot water until dough doubles in size, about 45 minutes.

Punch down dough and knead once more. Divide dough into 4 parts; divide each part into 8 to 10 pieces. Cover and let dough rise 1 to 1½ hours until dough looks light. Steam over boiling water for 20 minutes. Makes 36 to 40.

Note: Use this dough for Cha-Shu Bao Tzu, Dow Sa Bao Tzu, Chinese Mushroom Bao Tzu, Sausage Rolls, and Eight Precious Glutinous Roll, and Beef with Preserved Mustard Greens Bao Tzu. Bao Tzu can be frozen and resteamed for 25 minutes before serving. Half of this dough can be used for Dow Sa Bao Tzu and half for Sausage Rolls.

EIGHT PRECIOUS INGREDIENTS GLUTINOUS ROLLS

2 c.	glutinous (sweet) rice	500 mL
6	Chinese dried mushrooms	6
2 T.	dried shrimps	30 mL
2	Chinese sausages	2
1 recipe	Bao Tzu Dough	1 recipe
2 T.	vegetable oil	30 mL
½ c.	Virginia ham, chopped	125 mL
1 c.	chopped bamboo shoots	250 mL
1 stalk	scallion, chopped	1 stalk
½ c.	roast pork, chopped	125 mL
2–3 T.	soy sauce, to taste	30–45 mL
½–1 t.	salt, to taste	2–5 mL

Prepare in advance: Soak the rice in hot water for 2 hours. Soak the mushrooms and shrimps in warm water for 15 to 30 minutes until soft, then chop. Cut sausages into small pieces. Divide dough into 10 portions; roll each into 6 × 8-in. (15.2 × 20.3-cm) rectangles.

To make the filling: Drain the rice; steam over boiling water for 25 minutes; cool. Heat oil in a wok; add the next 4 ingredients and stir-fry for 1 minute. Add the rice and mix well. Add soy sauce and salt; stir until well mixed. Cool and use when ready to stuff the rolls.

To stuff, fill dough rectangles with the filling mixture; roll into 10 8-in. (20.3-cm)-long rolls; let rise a second time. Cut each roll into 4 to 6 pieces. Steam over boiling water for 25 minutes. Serve hot. Steamed rolls can be frozen and resteamed prior to serving. Makes 40 to 60.

CHICKEN MUSHROOM BAO TZU

冬菇鸡饱

½ lb.	boneless chicken breast	225 g
4 slices	fresh ginger	4 slices
1 stalk	scallion	1 stalk
8	Chinese dried mushrooms	8
½ t.	soy sauce	2 mL
2 T.	oyster sauce	30 mL
1 t.	sugar	5 mL
1 T.	cornstarch	15 mL
¼ c.	mushroom water	60 mL
½–1 t.	salt, to taste	2–5 mL
6 T.	vegetable oil	90 mL
1 c.	bamboo shoots, coarsely chopped	250 mL
1 recipe	Bao Tzu Dough	1 recipe

Dice the chicken breast. Chop ginger and scallion. Rinse mushrooms; cover with warm water and soak until soft, about 30 minutes. Drain and chop; save water. Mix the next 6 ingredients and set aside. Heat the oil. Add the ginger and scallion; stir-fry for 15 seconds. Add mushrooms; stir-fry for 15 seconds. Stir in the chicken and continue stir-frying for 1 minute. Add shoots, mix well and cook for 2 to 3 more minutes. Stir in the cornstarch mixture to thicken the filling. Cool thoroughly.

Stuff Bao Tzu Dough like Cha-Shu Bao Tzu but place the dumpling top down on wax paper so that the top looks smooth. Let the stuffed bao rise 45 minutes to 1 hour in warm place without draft until light and almost double the size. Steam over boiling water for 25 minutes. Makes 36 to 40.

CHA-SHU BAO TZU

义烧饱

¼ c.	sauce from roast pork	60 mL
3 T.	soy sauce	45 mL
2 T.	cornstarch	30 mL
2 T.	peanut butter or 2 t. (10 mL) sesame oil	30 mL
½–1 T.	sugar	7.5–15 mL
4 c.	roast pork, diced	1 L
1 recipe	Bao Tzu Dough	1 recipe

To make the filling, combine sauces, cornstarch, peanut butter, and sugar in a saucepan; cook over medium heat until thickened. Add the pork, mixing well. Cool filling before stuffing the dough.

Flatten each piece of dough with your hands into 3-in. (7.6-cm)-round patties. Place 1 T. (15 mL) of the mixture on each patty. Make pleats around edge and gather at the middle. Press together and seal top. Arrange dumplings on 2½-in. (6.4-cm)-square pieces of wax paper. Let rise 1 to 1½ hours until dough looks light. Steam over boiling water for 20 minutes. Steamed dumplings can be frozen and resteamed 15 minutes before serving. Cha-Shu Bao Tzu can also be baked (recipe follows). Serve hot. Makes 36 to 40.

BAKED CHA-SHU BAO TZU

焗饱

1 recipe	Cha-Shu Bao Tzu	1 recipe
1	egg	1
2 t.	water	10 mL
½ t.	sugar	2 mL
	margarine or butter, melted	

Place dumplings 2 in. (5.1 cm) apart on a cookie sheet, upside down on a piece of wax paper; beat egg and combine with water and sugar; mix well. Brush on the dumplings. Bake at 350 °F (175 °C) for 20 to 25 minutes until golden brown. Brush with melted margarine. Baked Cha-Shu Bao Tzu can be frozen. To serve, thaw and wrap in foil; reheat at 325 °F (165 °C) for 25 minutes. Makes 36 to 40.

DOW SA BAO TZU

豆沙飽

Use half the Bao Tzu Dough recipe and 1 lb. (450 g) bean paste (dow sa) for the filling to make 20 Dow Sa Bao Tzu. Bean paste is available in Chinese pastry shops. Makes about 20.

SAUSAGE ROLLS

臘腸捲

| 1 recipe | Bao Tzu Dough | 1 recipe |
| 10 | Chinese pork sausages, cut into halves | 10 |

Flatten dough into 2½-in. (6.4-cm)-diameter pieces with your hand. Place sausage in middle; fold dough over, leaving ends open. Place the folded side down on a 2½-in. (6.4-cm) square piece of wax paper. Let rise for 1 to 1½ hours. Steam over boiling water for 25 minutes. These rolls can be frozen and resteamed for 15 minutes before serving. Serve warm. Makes 36 to 40.

BEEF WITH PRESERVED MUSTARD GREENS BAO TZU

牛肉咸菜飽

Mustard greens are known as *hom tsoi* in Cantonese and *shien tsai* in Mandarin.

1 recipe	Bao Tzu Dough	1 recipe
1 lb.	ground beef chuck	450 g
1½ c.	preserved mustard greens, chopped	375 mL
1½ c.	bamboo shoots	375 mL
1 T.	soy sauce	15 mL
1 t.	salt	5 mL
¼ t.	MSG (optional)	1 mL
1 t.	sesame oil	5 mL
1 T.	scallion, chopped	15 mL
1 t.	fresh ginger, chopped	5 mL

Mix all the ingredients except the dough; use as filling for the dough. Follow Cha-Shu Bao Tzu directions to make and stuff these dumplings. Steam over boiling water for 25 minutes. Serve hot.

MUNG BEAN SWEET SOUP

綠豆粥

1 c.	mung beans	250 mL
1–2 pieces	dried tangerine peel (tsen pi) (optional)	1–2 pieces
1–2 pieces	Chinese brown sugar, to taste	1–2 pieces

Cover beans with water; discard those that float. Wash and drain. Rinse the tangerine peel. Place beans and peel in a pot. Add 1½ qts. (1½ L) water. Bring to a boil; lower the heat and cook for 45 minutes to 1 hour. Add brown sugar, stirring until dissolved. Serve hot or cold.

Note: Soup may be kept in refrigerator for a few days. To make Mung Bean Soup with Coconut Milk, omit the tangerine peels, add ½ to 1 c. (125 to 250 mL) coconut milk with the sugar. Bring back to a boil. Serve hot.

MO SHU PORK (Mo Shu Ro)

½ lb.	pork, shredded	225 g
2 t.	cornstarch	10 mL
1 T.	soy sauce	15 mL
½ t.	sugar	2 mL
4	Chinese dried mushrooms	4
1 T.	cloud ears	15 mL
12–15	golden lilies	12–15
½ c.	bamboo shoots, shredded	125 mL
5 T.	vegetable oil	75 mL
2–3	eggs, beaten	2–3
½ c.	water chestnuts, shredded	125 mL
1 T.	soy sauce	15 mL
½ t.	sugar	2 mL
½ t.	salt	2 mL
1 stalk	scallion, chopped	1 stalk
1 recipe	Bo Bing (Pancakes)	1 recipe

Mix the first 4 ingredients; marinate for 15 minutes. Rinse the mushrooms, cloud ears, and lilies; soak in separate bowls of warm water for 15 to 25 minutes, or until soft; drain. Shred mushrooms thinly. Wash the cloud ears until clean, then shred. Cut lilies into ½-in. (13-mm) pieces.

To cook: Heat 2 T. (30 mL) of the oil and scramble the eggs; remove eggs to a warm dish. Heat remaining oil; add the pork mixture and stir-fry for 1 minute. Mix in the mushrooms, cloud ears, and lilies. Add the bamboo shoots and water chestnuts, stirring for 1 minute. Season with soy sauce and sugar. Mix in the salt, scallion, and eggs. Serve with Bo Bing.

BO BING (Pancakes)

2 c.	all-purpose flour	500 mL
⅔ c.	boiling water	180 mL
6 T.	cold water	90 mL
2 t.	sesame oil	10 mL

Place flour in a bowl; gradually add the boiling water, stirring with chopsticks until well mixed. Let stand a couple of minutes, then add the cold water. Knead until dough is smooth and elastic. Cover with a piece of cloth and let stand for 10 minutes. Remove dough to floured board and knead again; divide dough into 2 parts. Roll 1 part into a long roll; divide into 12 parts. Roll each part into a ball, then flatten each with hands. Lightly brush surface of 1 piece with sesame oil; place second piece on top. Pat dough down a little and roll the double-layered piece very thin, about 6-in. (15.2 cm) in diameter. Repeat until 24 pancakes are made.

Cook pancake in heated ungreased skillet over medium heat for 30 seconds; turn over and heat for 30 seconds. Turn pancake over to a dish, separating the double pancake into 2. Cover with clean cloth. Pancakes can be prepared in advance and refrigerated. To serve, reheat by steaming in a steamer for 5 minutes. Serve with Mo Shu Ro. Makes 48.

SHREDDED CHICKEN LO MEIN

鸡絲捞麵

1	chicken breast	1
2 t.	soy sauce	10 mL
2 t.	cornstarch	10 mL
1 T.	sherry	15 mL
½ t.	sugar	2 mL
1 t.	vegetable oil	5 mL
4	Chinese dried mushrooms	4
3	carrots, about ½ lb. (225 g)	3
½ lb.	fresh noodles or spaghetti	225 g
¼ c.	vegetable oil	60 mL
4 c.	cabbage, shredded, about ½ lb. (225 g)	1 L
3 stalks	celery, shredded	3 stalks
½ t.	salt and black pepper, to taste	2 mL
1–2 T.	soy sauce, to taste	15–30 mL

Slice, then shred the chicken breast; mix with soy sauce, cornstarch, sherry, sugar, and 1 t. (5 mL) oil. Rinse mushrooms, cover with warm water and soak for 30 minutes until soft; drain and shred. Scrape the carrots; cut diagonally into thin slices; shred. Cook noodles in boiling water for 3 to 5 minutes or until the desired tenderness; drain in a colander; rinse under cold water. Heat ¼ c. (60 mL) oil in a wok; add the marinated chicken and stir-fry 1 to 2 minutes. Remove to a dish; pour excess oil back into wok. Turn up the heat; add mushrooms and stir-fry a few seconds. Add carrots, cabbage, and celery, stirring well for 2 minutes. Cover and cook for 2 minutes more. Add cooked noodles to the chicken mixture, mixing well. Season with salt, pepper, and soy sauce. Stir well and serve.

ROAST PORK LO MEIN (Cha-Shu Lo Mein)

6	Chinese dried mushrooms (optional)	6
½ lb.	fresh noodles or dry thin spaghetti	225 g
4 T.	vegetable oil	60 mL
1 clove	garlic, chopped	1 clove
1	scallion, cut into 1-in. (2.5-cm)-long pieces	1
1 c.	roast pork, cooked beef, chicken, or turkey	250 mL
2	carrots, shredded	2
2 stalks	celery, shredded	2 stalks
4 c.	cabbage, shredded	1 L
2 T.	soy sauce	30 mL
½ t.	salt and black pepper	2 mL

Soak mushrooms in warm water for 15 minutes or until soft; shred. If fresh noodles are used, follow Cantonese Chow Mein instructions to prepare noodles. If using spaghetti, add spaghetti to 2 qts. (2 L) boiling water; stir well. When water boils again, turn off heat. Cover and let spaghetti remain in pot for 15 to 18 minutes; drain. Heat oil in a wok; add garlic and scallion; stir-fry for 15 seconds. Add the pork; stir-fry for 1 minute. Remove to a dish, pouring excess oil back into wok. Add carrots, celery, cabbage, and mushrooms to the wok, stirring well for 1 to 2 minutes. Cover and cook 2 more minutes. Add noodles or spaghetti and the pork mixture; mix well. Season to your taste with soy sauce, salt, and pepper. Stir well and serve.

CURRIED JAO WRAPPERS

咖喱角

3½ c.	all-purpose flour	875 mL
1¼ c.	vegetable shortening, lard, or Crisco	310 mL
¾ c.	warm water	190 mL
1 recipe	Curried Jao Filling (recipe follows)	1 recipe

Mix 1 c. (250 mL) of the flour with ½ c. (125 mL) shortening; divide into 4 parts; roll each part into a ball. Mix remaining flour and shortening and the water; divide into 4 parts. Roll 1 part into a round pancake. Wrap dough pancake around a dough ball. With rolling pin, roll it out into an oblong piece on a lightly floured board. Roll it up like a jelly roll, then flatten it and roll into an oblong shape again. Repeat the rolling once more, 90° in another direction. Cut each roll into 8 pieces; flatten each piece and roll into 3 to 3½-in (7.6 to 8.9-cm)-round wrappers (32 wrappers). Fill each wrapper with the filling; fold into half-moon shapes. Brush each with well-beaten egg. Bake on well-greased cookie sheet at 425 °F (220 °C) for 25 to 30 minutes. Serve hot or cold. Makes 32.

CURRIED JAO FILLING

咖喱角餡

½ lb.	ground chuck or round	225 g
1	red onion, about ¼ lb. (120 g), chopped	1
2–3 t.	curry powder, to taste	10–15 mL
1 T.	vinegar	15 mL
1 T.	soy sauce	15 mL
1½ t.	salt	7 mL
½ t.	sugar	2 mL
¼ t.	MSG (optional)	1 mL
1–2	potatoes, about ¼ lb. (120 g), cooked and mashed	1–2

Mix all ingredients together. Use as filling for the wrappers.

CURRIED CHICKEN RICE NOODLES

1½ lb.	chicken	675 g
1 medium	red onion	1 medium
1–2 cloves	garlic	1–2 cloves
2 medium	potatoes, about ½ lb. (240 g)	2 medium
½ lb.	rice noodles	225 g
3 T.	vegetable oil	45 mL
2–3 t.	curry powder	10–15 mL
1½ t.	salt	7 mL
2 c.	water	500 mL
7-oz. can	coconut milk	200-g can

Cut chicken into bite-sized pieces. Peel, quarter, and cut the onion into ¼-in. (6-mm) slices. Pound the garlic with flat side of cleaver; remove skin and chop garlic. Peel potatoes and cut into bite-sized pieces. Cook the noodles in boiling water for 3 to 5 minutes; drain and keep warm, or to heat, pour hot water over noodles and drain just before serving.

Heat the oil in a wok and brown the onion and garlic for 1 minute. Season to your taste with curry powder and salt, mixing well. Add the chicken; stir-fry for 3 minutes. Stir in the water, bring to a boil, lower heat and simmer for 10 minutes. Add the coconut milk and potatoes; cook 10 minutes longer. Place cooked noodles on a warm serving dish; pour the chicken mixture over noodles. Serve hot.

DRUNKEN CHICKEN

2–3 lbs.	fryer	1–1.5 K
1–2 t.	salt	5–10 mL
6 slices	fresh ginger	6 slices
1 stalk	scallion	1 stalk
1 c.	dry sherry or Chinese shao-shing wine	250 mL

Rinse the chicken; pat dry with paper towel; quarter. Rub chicken with salt. Add the ginger. Split scallion in half lengthwise; cut across into 3 to 4 segments. Mix scallion with the chicken; refrigerate for 2 days.

When ready to cook, place chicken in a single layer in a bowl. Cover with plastic wrap. Steam in a bowl over boiling water until cooked, about 30 minutes. Remove chicken from bowl; cool in a clean bowl. Strain broth remaining in the bowl. Add sherry to broth and pour over chicken pieces, turning them until each piece is coated. Cover and refrigerate for at least one day; turn chicken pieces over once or twice. Drain off marinating liquid and reserve for cooking. Cut chicken into bite-sized pieces and serve cold.

CHICKEN ROLLS

¾ lb.	chicken white meat, minced	340 g
1	egg	1
1 T.	scallion, chopped	15 mL
1 t.	fresh ginger, chopped	5 mL
1 t.	salt	5 mL
½ t.	sugar	2 mL
¼ t.	MSG (optional)	1 mL
1 c.	water chestnuts, finely chopped	250 mL
	black pepper, to taste	
12 slices	thin-sliced fresh soft bread	12 slices
3 c.	peanut oil	750 mL

Combine the first 8 ingredients and season with pepper, mixing thoroughly. Cut off crusts of the bread; press down on each bread slice with roller until firm. Spread chicken mixture on top of each bread slice and roll up.

To cook: Heat oil in a wok to 300 °F (150 °C). Deep-fry the rolls, 4 at a time, until golden brown, about 5 to 8 minutes. Serve hot.

ANGELA'S SUGAR & SPICE NUTS

3 c.	unsalted mixed nuts	750 mL
1	egg white	1
1 T.	orange juice or water	15 mL
⅔ c.	sugar	180 mL
1 t.	ground cinnamon	5 mL
½ t.	ground ginger	2 mL
½ t.	ground allspice	2 mL
¼ t.	salt	1 mL

Place nuts in a large bowl; set aside. In a small bowl, beat egg white and orange juice until frothy. Add remaining ingredients, mixing well; pour over the nuts and coat well. Spread nuts on a cookie sheet. Bake at 275 °F (135 °C), stirring every 15 minutes, until light brown and crisp, about 45 to 55 minutes; cool. Store in airtight container in a cool place for up to 1 month.

CANTONESE CHOW MEIN

In Canton (Kwangtung) chow mein noodles are pan-browned on both sides; then the meat, vegetables and sauce are poured on top of the noodles before the dish is served. In North China, this dish is called *liang man hwang* (meaning "both sides brown"). These dishes contrast with Cantonese lo mein where the noodles are first boiled and then stir-fried with the vegetables and meat without browning them.

½ lb.	pork, chicken or beef	225 g
2 t.	cornstarch	10 mL
2 t.	soy sauce	10 mL
1 T.	dry sherry	15 mL
1 t.	vegetable oil	5 mL
6	Chinese dried mushrooms	6
½ lb.	fresh noodles	225 g
2 t.	vegetable oil or sesame oil	10 mL
½ c.	peanut oil	125 mL
1 clove	garlic, chopped	1 clove
1 stalk	scallion, cut into 1½-in. (3.8-cm)-long pieces	1 stalk
1 t.	salt	5 mL
1 c.	soup stock	250 mL
1 c.	bamboo shoots, shredded	250 mL
2	carrots, shredded	2
1½ T.	cornstarch	22.5 mL
2 T.	water	30 mL

Slice the meat, then shred; mix with the next 4 ingredients. Rinse the mushrooms, cover with warm water and soak for 30 minutes until soft; shred.

To cook the noodles, drop in boiling water, stirring with chopsticks for 3 to 5 minutes or until the desired tenderness. Drain in a colander and rinse under cold water. Drain well, place in a bowl and add 2 t. (10 mL) oil, stirring well.

Heat 3 T. (45 mL) of the peanut oil in a skillet over medium heat; add the noodles, spreading them like a pancake; cook until bottom browns, about 2 to 3 minutes. Turn noodles over, add 2 T. (30 mL) of the peanut oil along edge of skillet and fry until noodles are brown; remove to a hot platter. Heat remaining peanut oil; add the marinated meat, garlic, and scallion, stirring well for 1 minute. Add the mushrooms, shoots, and carrots; stir well for 2 minutes. Sprinkle the salt and add the stock, mixing well; cover pan and cook for 2 more minutes. Mix the cornstarch and water; stir into the mixture. Cook until thickened. Spread mixture over the warm noodles and serve.

FIVE SPICES TEA EGG

12	eggs	12
½ c.	soy sauce	125 mL
½ c.	red tea leaves	125 mL
1 T.	salt	15 mL
1 T.	five spices powder	15 mL

Combine all ingredients in a saucepan; add enough water to cover and cook 10 minutes. Gently crack eggshells so that sauce and flavor can penetrate but shells do not disintegrate. Bring to a boil; then lower heat and simmer for 20 minutes; cool.

BOILED DUMPLINGS

水餃

2½ c.	all-purpose flour	625 mL
¼ t.	salt	1 mL
1 c.	cold water	250 mL
1 lb.	Chinese celery cabbage	450 g
¾ lb.	ground beef or pork	340 g
1 stalk	scallion, chopped	1 stalk
1 t.	fresh ginger, chopped	5 mL
2 T.	soy sauce	30 mL
½ t.	sugar	2 mL
1 t.	salt	5 mL
½ t.	sesame oil	2 mL
1 T.	peanut oil	15 mL

Place flour in a mixing bowl; dissolve salt in the water and gradually add to the flour. Mix well with fingers and knead until dough is soft and elastic. Form dough in a ball and cover with a damp cloth; let stand for 15 minutes. Chop cabbage and sprinkle with ½ t. (2 mL) salt; mix well, then squeeze out the water. To make the filling, mix the cabbage with the remaining ingredients; beat until smooth and elastic.

Remove dough to floured board; knead once and divide into 4 portions. Cut each portion into 12 pieces. Using hands, roll each piece into a little ball, then flatten balls with hands; roll into 2½-in. (6.4-cm)-round pieces with a rolling pin; roll edge thinner than middle. Place 1 T. (15 mL) of the filling in middle of each round; fold over, seal edges, and pinch in middle; gather one side to form a canoe and stretch it gently so that it looks like a little boat.

To cook the dumplings, bring 2 qts. (2 L) water to a boil; drop dumplings 1 at a time into boiling water (about 15 to 20 in each batch). Stir gently and cover; cook until water boils again. Add ⅔ c. (180 mL) cold water to pan; cook until water boils again. Repeat the addition of cold water. When it boils again dumplings are done. Serve dumplings with soy sauce mixed with vinegar, hot pepper, oil, or even with finely chopped garlic. Makes 48.

CANTONESE STEAMED EGG

蒸蛋

½ oz.	cellophane noodles (fun-see)	15 g
4	Chinese dried mushrooms	4
6	dried shrimps	6
1 T.	dry sherry	15 mL
2–3	eggs	2–3
¾ t.	salt	4 mL
1 T.	scallions, chopped	15 mL
½–1 t.	sesame oil, to taste	2–5 mL
1 t.	soy sauce	5 mL

Cover noodles with hot water and soak for 30 to 45 minutes; drain and cut into 1- to 2-in. (2.5 to 5.1 cm)-long segments. Rinse mushrooms; soak in warm water for 30 minutes; drain, reserving water and chop. Clean and rinse the shrimps under cold water; soak in sherry for 30 minutes, then chop. Beat eggs well; mix in the noodle mixture and 1 c. (250 mL) mushroom water. Steam over boiling water for 15 minutes. Sprinkle scallion, sesame oil, and soy sauce on top and serve. Cool and serve plain or with a favorite sauce.

FRIED DUMPLINGS

锅贴

3 c.	all-purpose flour	750 mL
¾ c.	boiling water	190 mL
6 T.	cold water	90 mL
6	Chinese black mushrooms	6
¾ lb.	Chinese celery cabbage	340 g
1 lb.	ground pork	450 g
1 stalk	scallion, chopped	1 stalk
1 t.	fresh ginger, chopped	5 mL
½ t.	sugar	2 mL
2 T.	soy sauce	30 mL
1 T.	sesame oil	15 mL
1½ t.	salt	7 mL
1½ T.	vegetable oil	22.5 mL
⅔ c.	hot water	180 mL
½ t.	vinegar	2 mL
few drops	sesame oil	few drops

To make the dough, pour flour into a mixing bowl and gradually add the boiling water, mixing well with chopsticks. Let mixture stand for 5 minutes. Add the cold water and mix well, kneading until dough becomes soft and elastic. Shape into a ball and cover with a cloth. Let dough stand 15 minutes. Place dough on floured board and knead until smooth. Divide dough into 48 pieces; roll each piece into a ball, then press flat. Cover with a cloth until ready to stuff dumplings.

To make the filling, soak the mushrooms in warm water about 30 minutes or until soft; discard stems and chop the mushroom caps. Parboil cabbage in boiling water for 2 minutes; rinse cabbage under cold water, squeeze out the water and chop cabbage very finely. In a bowl, mix the pork, mushrooms, cabbage, scallion, ginger, sugar, soy sauce, sesame oil, and salt. Place 1 T. (15 mL) of the filling on the middle of each dough circle; fold over to make a half circle, gathering the sides and pressing edges together to seal.

To cook, heat skillet and add the vegetable oil. When hot, add enough dumplings to cover bottom of pan, starting from inside of pan along the edge and arranging in a circular pattern. Cook over medium heat until bottom of dumplings are golden brown, about 2 minutes. Mix the hot water, vinegar, and few drops sesame oil. Add to the pan; cover and steam dumplings until water is all absorbed, about 5 minutes. Add an additional 1 T. (15 mL) vegetable oil along pan edges and cook for another minute. Cover pan with a serving dish; invert pan so that the golden brown side of dumpling is on top. Serve with vinegar and soy sauce or hot sauce. Dumplings can be frozen and reheated. Makes 48.

SHRIMP FRIED DUMPLINGS

虾锅贴

dough from 1 recipe	Fried Dumplings	dough from 1 recipe
½ lb.	ground pork	225 g
1 T.	scallion, chopped	15 mL
4 slices	fresh ginger, chopped	4 slices
2 T.	light soy sauce	30 mL
1 t.	sesame oil	5 mL
¼ lb.	shrimps	120 g
1 t.	wine	5 mL
1 t.	cornstarch	5 mL
½ t.	salt	2 mL

1 lb.	Chinese celery cabbage	450 g
3 T.	oil	45 mL
½ c.	chicken broth	125 mL

Make the dough and shape into dough circles. Cover with a cloth until ready to stuff the dumplings. To make the filling, combine the pork, scallion, ginger, soy sauce, and sesame oil. Shell and devein the shrimp; wash, dry, then mince the shrimp. Mix shrimp with wine, cornstarch, and salt; add to the filling. Parboil the cabbage, drain, and finely chop; add to the filling and mix well. To stuff and cook the dumplings, follow directions for Fried Dumplings. Makes 48.

INSTANT LO MEIN

伊府拐麵

1 c.	boiling water	250 mL
1 pkg.	instant noodles	1 pkg.
	soup base from package noodles or 1 beef bouillon cube	
½–1 c.	cooked Virginia ham, roast turkey, chicken, or roast pork, shredded	125–250 mL
½–1 c.	lettuce heart, shredded	125–250 mL
1 T.	scallions, chopped	15 mL
	sesame oil, to taste	

In a saucepan with the water boiling, drop the noodles, stirring and separating with chopsticks; cook until water is soaked up, about 2 minutes. Add the soup base, stirring well. Stir in the remaining ingredients; mix well and serve.

SWEET & SOUR LOTUS ROOT

甜酸藕片

½ lb.	lotus roots	225 g
1½ T.	peanut oil	22.5 mL
3 T.	sugar	45 mL
2 T.	vinegar	30 mL
¼ t.	salt	1 mL

Peel and cut lotus roots crosswise into very thin slices. Place slices in 3 c. (750 mL) boiling water; cook for ½ minute when water boils again. Drain and place in a dish. Mix remaining ingredients in a saucepan; cook for 1 to 2 minutes, stirring constantly. Pour over lotus slices, mix well and serve.

PEARL MEATBALLS

珍珠丸子

½ c.	glutinous (sweet) rice	125 mL
10	dried shrimps	10
8	water chestnuts	8
½ lb.	ground pork	225 g
1 T.	scallion, chopped	15 mL
½ t.	sugar	2 mL
¾ t.	salt, to taste	4 mL
2 t.	soy sauce	10 mL

Cover rice with hot water and soak for 2 hours; drain. Clean shrimps; soak in warm water for 15 minutes. Chop the water chestnuts. Combine pork, shrimps, and water chestnuts with all ingredients except rice; mix well. Shape into about 15 walnut-sized balls. Roll each meatball over moist rice until well coated. Arrange meatballs in a single layer on a dish. Steam over boiling water for 30 minutes. Serve hot.

SHRIMP GO-TE (Chinese Pan-Browned Ravioli)

蝦鍋貼

10-oz. pkg.	frozen chopped spinach	283-g pkg.
4 oz.	shrimps, shelled, deveined and minced	120 g
½ lb.	ground pork	225 g
1 t.	fresh ginger, chopped	5 mL
2 stalks	scallion	2 stalks
1 T.	light soy sauce, to taste	15 mL
1½ t.	dry sherry	7 mL
2 t.	sesame oil	10 mL
1 t.	cornstarch	5 mL
½ t.	salt, to taste	2 mL
½ t.	sugar	2 mL
1 recipe	Go-Te Wrappers	1 recipe
6 T.	vegetable oil	90 mL
1 c.	chicken broth or water	250 mL

To make the filling, thaw the spinach; squeeze out water. In a bowl, combine spinach with next 10 ingredients; mix with hands until thoroughly mixed. Place about 1 t. (5 mL) of the filling in middle of each wrapper and fold over. Make 4 pleats along one side towards the middle; seal tightly with a little beaten egg or water. Repeat until all the filling has been used.

To cook, heat 3 T. (45 mL) of the oil in a skillet until it is very hot; turn off heat. Arrange dumplings in the pan in a circle. Heat for a few seconds over medium heat; check if bottoms are golden. Sprinkle ¼ c. (60 mL) broth or water over dumplings, cover tightly and lower heat; steam for 3 minutes. Repeat, adding more broth, until all liquid is absorbed. Turn off heat; remove cover. To remove dumplings, place a plate over skillet and invert over plate. Serve hot with wine vinegar and/or hot sauce. Shrimp Go-Te can be frozen. To reheat in skillet, add a little water and steam for a few minutes. Makes 60.

Note: You may follow the Shrimp Go-Te recipe and substitute ground pork or beef for the shrimp.

GO-TE OR SUEY GOW WRAPPERS

水餃皮

The same wrappers may be used for Go-Te or Suey Gow.

4 c.	all-purpose flour	1 L
1½ c.	hot (boiled) water	375 mL
1½ T.	vegetable oil	22.5 mL

Place flour on pastry board; make a well in middle. Mix the water and oil and pour into the well. Mix thoroughly, kneading until dough is smooth and elastic. Divide dough into 6 portions. Remove 1 portion; cover remainder with a piece of damp cloth while working on each portion. Knead, roll each portion into a long roll, then cut into 10 pieces. Roll each piece into a ball, then roll ball out into a 2.5-in. (6.4-cm) circle. Fill each circle with 1 t. (5 mL) filling. Repeat procedure until all dough is used. Makes 60.

Note: Wrappers for Go-Te or Suey Gow are available in any Chinese grocery shop for a very reasonable price, if you prefer to buy them.

BEEF SUEY GOW

牛肉水餃

¼ lb.	beef	120 g
10-oz. pkg.	frozen chopped kale or spinach, thawed and squeezed	283-g pkg.
2 stalks	scallion, chopped	2 stalks

6 slices	fresh ginger, chopped	6 slices
1 clove	garlic, chopped	1 clove
1 T.	sherry	15 mL
1 T.	soy sauce	15 mL
2 t.	sesame oil	10 mL
½ t.	sugar	2 mL
½ t.	salt, to taste	2 mL
2 T.	chicken broth or soup stock	30 mL
1-lb. pkg.	Suey Gow Wrappers	450-g pkg.

Combine all ingredients except the wrappers, mixing thoroughly by hand. Place about 1 t. (5 mL) of the mixture in middle of each wrapper and fold over. Along 1 side, make 4 pleats towards the middle; seal tightly with a little beaten egg or water. Drop in boiling water for 2 minutes. When dumplings are cooked, they float to top. Serve hot with vinegar and soy sauce and/or hot sauce. Makes 40.

ANISE PEPPER-SALT SHRIMP BALL

椒盐蝦球

1 lb.	fresh shrimps	450 g
2 oz.	fatty pork	60 g
1 t.	salt	5 mL
1 T.	dry sherry	15 mL
6 slices	fresh ginger	6 slices
2 T.	cold water	30 mL
1	egg white	1
2 stalks	scallion, finely chopped	2 stalks
3 T.	cornstarch	45 mL
2 c.	peanut oil	500 mL
	Anise Pepper-Salt for dipping (recipe follows)	

Shell and devein shrimps; wash with cold water and pat dry with paper towel. Flatten with side of cleaver and chop until mushy. Finely chop the pork. Combine shrimps and pork in a bowl. Add salt and sherry; mix well. Shred ginger, chop and soak in water for 10 minutes; drain and save ginger liquid, discarding the ginger. Add ginger liquid to shrimp, one third at a time, beating well. Beat egg white until stiff; add to shrimp mixture. Add scallion and cornstarch; mix thoroughly.

Heat oil to the smoking point, then reduce to low heat and keep oil at 250 °F (120 °C). Wet left hand and place about ¼ c. (60 mL) of the mixture in your palm; close fingers and squeeze out walnut-sized amount of mixture from the top of your fist. Remove ball preferably with wet china spoon, and drop it in the heated oil; fry until golden brown and crispy, about 3 to 4 minutes. As balls rise to surface, separate them with chopsticks; drain on paper towel. Serve hot with Anise Pepper-Salt.

Note: Shrimp balls can be prepared a day ahead and stored in refrigerator before deep-frying.

ANISE PEPPER-SALT

椒盐

1 T.	anise peppercorns	15 mL
3 T.	salt	45 mL

Stir-fry anise peppercorns over low heat in an ungreased, dry skillet until it is dark brown and fragrant. Add salt, and continue stirring until salt is a little brown, about 1 minute. Remove to a dish; cool. Grind until very fine. Store indefinitely in a tightly covered bottle. Use as a dip for roasted or fried meat dishes.

HAR GOW (Shrimp Dumplings)

蝦餃

This recipe includes Har Gow dumpling wrappers and the filling.

1½ c.	wheat starch	375 mL
½ c.	tapioca flour	125 mL
dash	salt	dash
1½ c.	boiling water	375 mL
1 T.	lard or vegetable oil	15 mL
1 lb.	fresh shrimps, shelled, deveined, chopped	450 g
1 T.	sherry	15 g
1 small can	water chestnuts, chopped	1 small can
1 t.	fresh ginger, chopped	5 mL
1 T.	scallion, chopped	15 mL
½ t.	sugar	2 mL
2 t.	soy sauce	10 mL
1–2 t.	sesame oil	5–10 mL
	salt, to taste	
dash	black pepper	dash

To make the dough, sift the starch, flour, and salt into a bowl. Pour boiling water over the flour mixture and mix well with chopsticks. Let stand for 5 to 10 minutes; knead until dough is smooth and elastic, about 2 minutes. Add lard or oil and knead again, until well mixed. Divide dough into 4 parts; roll each part with hands into long cylinder. Cut each cylinder into 10 to 11 pieces. Roll each piece into a ball and flatten with cleaver to make wrappers 2½ in. (6.4 cm) in diameter.

Combine remaining ingredients and mix well for the filling. Fill each dumpling with 1 to 1½ t. (5 to 7 mL) of the filling. Repeat until all the filling is used up. Pleat or gather into ½ in. (13 mm) basket shapes, closed at the top. Place dumplings in a well-greased round cake pan (each pan holds 20); or line plate or cake pan with large lettuce leaves before adding the *har gow*. Steam over boiling water for 10 minutes. Serve with hoisin sauce. Makes 40 to 44.

FUN GOH

粉果

6	Chinese mushrooms	6
1 T.	vegetable oil	15 mL
½ lb.	ground pork	225 g
½ c.	water chestnuts, chopped, or Chinese cabbage, chopped	125 mL
½ t.	sugar	2 mL
½ t.	salt	2 mL
2 t.	cornstarch	10 mL
1 T.	soy sauce	15 mL
1 t.	sherry	5 mL
	pepper	
1 T.	scallion, chopped	15 mL
1 recipe	Har Gow dumpling wrappers	1 recipe

Rinse the mushrooms; soak in warm water for 30 minutes or until soft. Discard stem and chop finely. Heat the oil in a wok. Add the pork, mushrooms, water chestnuts or cabbage; stir-fry for 1 minute. Add sugar and salt, mixing well. Mix the cornstarch, soy sauce, sherry, and pepper. Add to the pork mixture, stirring until thickened. Stir in the scallion and mix well; cool. Place 1 to 2 t. (5 to 10 mL) of the mixture in middle of each wrapper. Fold over into shape of half-moon and press to seal. Arrange Fun Goh in a single layer on a greased plate. Steam over boiling water for 10 minutes. Makes 40 to 44.

YEE FUN MEIN (Instant Noodles)　　　　　　　伊府麵

Instant noodles were created by the House of Yee in Canton. Now all varieties of instant noodles are available in 3-oz. (85-g) packages in grocery stores or supermarkets. They are easy to prepare, and leftover meats and a few leaves of vegetables can be added to create a substantial lunch or snack.

INSTANT NOODLES WITH SOUP　　　　　　　　伊府湯麵

2 c.	water	500 mL
1–2 c.	celery cabbage or cabbage, cut bite-sized	250–500 mL
1 pkg.	instant noodles	1 pkg.
½ c.	leftover meat (roast chicken, pork, beef, or others), shredded	125 mL
	soup base from noodle package or 2 chicken bouillon cubes	
1 T.	scallion, chopped	15 mL

Bring water to a boil. Add cabbage and cook for 2 to 3 minutes. Stir in the noodles, separating with chopsticks. Add the meat and soup base; mix well. Garnish with scallion and serve.

CHA-SHU ROAST PORK

2 lbs.	boneless pork	900 g
2 stalks	scallion	2 stalks
3 T.	dry sherry	45 mL
2 T.	soy sauce	30 mL
4 T.	sugar	60 mL
1 T.	hoisin sauce	15 mL
2 t.	brown bean sauce	10 mL
1–1½ t.	salt, to taste	5–7 mL
4–6 slices	fresh ginger	4–6 slices
1 T.	vegetable oil	15 mL

Cut pork into strips 6 in. (15.2 cm) long and 1½ in. (3.8 cm) wide; cut 3 to 4 slashes on each side about ¼ in. (6-mm) deep. Pound scallion with side of cleaver; cut each into 2-in. (5.1-cm) long pieces. Mix all ingredients except pork in a large bowl; add pork strips and marinate for 4 hours. Place pork on a cake rack set on a foil-lined baking pan. Pour 1 to 2 c. (250 to 500 mL) hot water on the pan. Bake at 350 °F (175 °C) for 25 minutes; then turn over and bake another 25 minutes. Turn heat up to 375 °F (190 °C) and bake 7 more minutes on each side. Serve as an appetizer, add to fried rice, omelette, noodles, or use as dumpling filling with Bao Dough.

EASY WAY TO PREPARE RICE

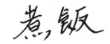

| 1 c. | long-grain rice | 250 mL |
| 1½ c. | cold water | 375 mL |

Place rice in a pot. Cover with cold water, wash, and discard the water. Repeat once or twice until water is nearly clear. Add 1½ c. (375 mL) cold water. Bring to a boil over high heat and cook for 2 minutes. When water is almost boiled down to rice level, cover tightly and turn heat as low as possible. Simmer for 15 minutes.

Note: Leftover rice can be reheated in a pot with small amount of water, ¼ c. (60 mL) water for about 2 bowls of rice. Cover tightly and warm over very low flame for 10 to 15 minutes, or place in a container and steam over boiling water for 5 to 10 minutes. Leftover rice also can be used for Yang Chow Fried Rice and other dishes.

YANG CHOW FRIED RICE

4	Chinese dried mushrooms	4
5 T.	vegetable oil	75 mL
1 T.	scallion, chopped	15 mL
1	Chinese sausage, diced (optional)	1
½ c.	shrimps, diced	125 mL
½ c.	roast pork or cooked ham, diced	125 mL
½ c.	frozen peas	125 mL
½ c.	bamboo shoots, diced	125 mL
2	eggs	2
4 c.	cold cooked rice	1 L
1½ T.	soy sauce	22.5 mL
	salt and pepper to taste	

Rinse mushrooms. Cover with warm water and soak for 30 minutes or until soft; chop. Heat 3 T. (45 mL) of the oil in a wok; add scallion and stir-fry a few seconds. Add sausage and shrimps. Stir-fry for 30 seconds. Add meat, peas, shoots, and mushrooms, stirring for 2 to 3 minutes. Put aside. Heat remaining oil; add the eggs and scramble. Stir in the rice and heat thoroughly. Combine with the meat and vegetables. Add seasonings, mix well and serve.

STEAMED RICE ROLLS (Tzu Tsang Fun)

10	dried shrimps, chopped (optional)	10
2 T.	scallion, chopped	30 mL
1½ c.	cake flour	375 mL
3 T.	wheat starch	45 mL
½ t.	salt	2 mL
4 T.	vegetable oil	60 mL
2½ c.	cold water	625 mL
½ c.	Cha-Shu Roast Pork, minced	125 mL
2 T.	Chinese parsley, chopped	30 mL
1 T.	sesame seeds, toasted	15 mL
	soy sauce and sesame oil, to taste	

Soak dried shrimps in a little water for 30 minutes; drain and chop. Combine cake flour, starch, and salt. Add oil and 2½ c. (625 mL) cold water, mixing well. Strain batter through a sieve into another bowl so that batter is smooth and free of lumps. Spoon about ⅓ c. (90 mL) of the batter into a greased 8-in. (20-cm) pie pan; sprinkle pork, shrimps, scallion, and parsley evenly over top. Steam over boiling water for 5 minutes. Remove from steamer; roll like a jelly roll; then sprinkle with toasted sesame seeds. Cut roll into 6 pieces; serve with individual dishes of soy sauce and sesame oil. Makes 24.

SHRIMP TOAST

蝦多士

1 lb.	frozen shrimps, minced	450 g
1 t.	fresh ginger, chopped	5 mL
1 T.	scallions, chopped	15 mL
1	egg	1
⅓ c.	all-purpose flour	90 mL
⅓ t.	baking powder	1.5 mL
2 t.	vegetable oil	10 mL
1½ t.	salt	7 mL
6½-oz. can	water chestnuts, minced	185-g can
14–15 slices	light brown toast	14–15 slices
	vegetable oil for deep frying	

Mix together all ingredients except toast and oil for frying. Spread shrimp mixture on the toast. Heat oil to 300 °F (150 °C). Fry toast with shrimp side down for 2 to 3 minutes. Turn toast over and fry half a minute more. Cut into 4 bite-sized pieces. Shrimp toast can be frozen and reheated at 375 °F (190 °C) for 10 minutes. Serve hot or cold.

JOAN'S FLUFFY SHRIMP

啤酒大蝦

12–15	jumbo shrimps	12–15
1	egg white	1
¼ c.	cornstarch	60 mL
6 T.	all-purpose flour	90 mL
½ t.	baking powder	2 mL
1 T.	vegetable oil or melted lard	15 mL
1–1½ t.	salt, to taste	5–7 mL
¼ c.	beer	60 mL
1½ c.	vegetable oil for frying	375 mL

Shell and devein shrimps; split, leaving them whole. Rinse and dry on paper towel. Beat egg white until fluffy. Gradually add remaining ingredients except beer and oil for frying, stirring constantly until batter is thoroughly mixed; stir in the beer. To fry, heat oil to 375 °F (190 °C), then lower to medium heat. Dip shrimps into batter and deep-fry 3 or 4 at a time, stirring and turning so that shrimps do not stick together, until shrimps are golden in color. Serve hot.

HOT MUSTARD GREENS
OR SZECHWAN CHUNG TSAI

1 T.	peanut oil	15 mL
1½ t.	salt	7 mL
1 T.	scallion, chopped	15 mL
1 t.	fresh ginger, chopped	5 mL
½ t.	anise peppercorns	2 mL
1 lb.	mustard green hearts, cut into bite-sized pieces	450 g

Heat oil over medium heat in a wok; add peppercorns, stirring until brown and fragrant, about 1 minute. Remove peppercorns from oil and discard. Turn heat up to high; add scallion and ginger; stir for a second. Add mustard greens and salt; stir-fry for 1½ minutes. Place cooked mustard greens in a container immediately; press down with a dish and cover tightly. When cool, store in refrigerator for 5 days before serving. Serve as an appetizer.

FOUR-COLOR SHU MAI

四色燒賣

1 recipe	Shu Mai Wrappers (recipe follows)	1 recipe
3/4 lb.	ground pork	340 g
1 c.	bamboo shoots, chopped	250 mL
1 t.	salt	5 mL
2 t.	cornstarch	10 mL
dash	black pepper	dash
1/2–1 T.	sesame oil	7.5–15 mL
4	black mushrooms	4
3 T.	dried shrimps	45 mL
3 T.	Virginia baked ham, chopped	45 mL
3 T.	spinach, chopped	45 mL

Prepare the wrappers according to the recipe. Keep covered with a damp towel while making the filling. Combine the pork and bamboo shoots with the next 4 ingredients, mixing thoroughly. Marinate while preparing the garnishes. Soak mushrooms in hot water until soft, about 15 to 30 minutes; discard stems and chop mushroom caps. Rinse shrimp and soak in warm water until soft; drain and chop.

To stuff and cook the dumplings: Place a small portion of the filling in each wrapper. Pinch sides of wrapper, forming a square with 4 holes. Garnish one hole with a little mushroom, another hole with shrimp, another with ham, and the last with spinach. Place dumplings in a steamer that has been lined with lettuce leaves or cheesecloth. Steam for 15 to 17 minutes over high heat. Serve hot with hoisin sauce. Makes 30.

SHU MAI WRAPPERS

燒賣皮

2 c.	all-purpose flour	500 mL
1/2 c.	boiling water	125 mL
1	egg	1

To make the wrappers: Place the flour in a bowl; slowly pour in the boiling water, stirring with chopsticks until well mixed. Add the egg and mix again. Knead mixture until smooth. Divide into 3 portions. Divide each portion into 10 pieces; shape each into a ball. Roll out each ball flat into 2 to 2 1/2-in. (5.1 to 6.4-cm) circles. You are now ready to stuff and cook the dumplings. Keep the dough covered with a damp towel. Makes 30.

GLUTINOUS RICE SHU MAI

糯米燒賣

1 c.	glutinous (sweet) rice	250 mL
6	Chinese dried mushrooms	6
4 oz.	ground pork	120 g
2 T.	soy sauce	30 mL
1 t.	cornstarch	5 mL
1/2 t.	sugar	2 mL
3 T.	peanut oil	45 mL
1 c.	bamboo shoots, chopped	250 mL
1/2 t.	MSG (optional)	2 mL
1 t.	salt	5 mL
1 recipe	Shu Mai Wrappers or 1 lb. (450 g) shu mai or won ton wrappers (with points cut off)	1 recipe
1 T.	dried shrimps, chopped	15 mL
2 T.	ham, chopped	30 mL

Cover rice with water; soak for half a day or overnight. Next day, drain rice. Rinse mushrooms, soak with warm water for 30 minutes until soft. Remove and discard stems; chop mushrooms. Mix pork with 1 T. (15 mL) of the soy sauce, the cornstarch, and the sugar. Heat oil in a wok; add mushrooms, pork mixture and shoots; stir-fry for 1 minute. Add the rice, remaining soy sauce, MSG, if using, and salt; stir well. Add ⅓ c. (90 mL) boiling water, mixing well. Place mixture in a bowl; steam over boiling water for 20 minutes.

To stuff: Hold hand in very loose fist; place wrapper between index finger and thumb and stuff with a small portion of the filling. Gather wrapper in at top to form a cup; sprinkle top of each dumpling with chopped shrimps and ham. Steam over boiling water for 8 minutes. Serve with hoisin sauce. Makes 30.

NONA'S SCALLION CREPES

This is a delicious and nutritious thin pancake to be eaten at breakfast or as a snack.

2	eggs	2
1 c.	flour	250 mL
½ t.	salt	2 mL
1 c.	skim milk	250 mL
2 T.	oil	30 mL
1–2 stalks	scallion, finely chopped	1–2 stalks
3 T.	sesame seeds (optional)	45 mL

Beat the eggs; add the salt, milk, and oil; mix well. Stir into the flour and beat until batter is well blended. Strain batter through a sieve into another bowl; stir in the scallion.

Heat a greased 7-in. (17-cm) nonstick pan. Add 1 ladleful batter, swirling it around. Sprinkle ¼ t. (1 mL) sesame seeds on each crepe. Cook over medium heat until light brown and the edges curl, about 1 to 1½ minutes. Turn over and cook for another ½ minute. Serve hot or cold. Makes 10 crepes.

SCALLION PANCAKES

3 c.	all-purpose flour	750 mL
1 c.	boiling water	250 mL
⅓ c.	cold water	90 mL
1½ T.	vegetable oil or melted lard	22.5 mL
3 t.	salt, to taste	15 mL
4 stalks	scallion, chopped	4 stalks
	peanut oil for frying	

Place flour in a bowl; gradually stir in the boiling water and mix well; let stand for 5 minutes. Slowly add cold water; knead until smooth and dough can be formed into a ball. Cover with wet towel and let stand for 15 minutes. Divide dough into 8 portions. Knead and roll each portion into thin pancakes about 10 in. (25.4 cm) in diameter (or slightly larger), then brush with ½ T. (7.5 mL) oil, sprinkle with ⅛ t. (.5 mL) salt and ½ T. (7.5 mL) scallion evenly on top. Roll pancake into a long roll with the ends tightly closed. Coil up the roll like a snail and tuck the end into the middle. Press roll with hand, then roll out into ¼-in. (6-mm) thin pancakes.

Heat 1 T. (15 mL) oil in a skillet over low heat. Add pancakes, cover and cook for 2 minutes. Turn pancakes over and add 1 T. (15 mL) oil around sides of pan. Cook until pancake is golden brown, lifting and shaking pan several times during cooking. Cut pancakes into 6 to 8 triangular pieces. Serve warm. Makes 48.

STEAMED SPARERIBS

1 lb.	spareribs	450 g
2 T.	dried fermented black beans	30 mL
1–2 cloves	garlic	1–2 cloves
1 T.	oil	15 mL
½–1 t.	salt, to taste	2–5 mL
1 t.	sugar	5 mL
1 T.	sherry	15 mL
1 T.	soy sauce	15 mL
1 T.	cornstarch	15 mL

Cut spareribs into 1 to 1½-in. (2.5 to 3.8-cm) pieces. Cover the beans with water, wash, drain, then chop. Using side of cleaver, pound garlic and remove skin; then chop finely. Heat oil in a wok; add the beans and garlic; stir-fry for ½ minute. Stir in the salt, sugar, sherry, and soy sauce, mixing well; turn off heat. Add sparerib pieces and mix well. Sprinkle cornstarch over spareribs and mix thoroughly. Place spareribs in a dish; cover lightly with plastic wrap. Steam over boiling water for 35 to 45 minutes. Serve hot.

SPARERIBS WITH SPECIAL SAUCE

1½ lbs.	spareribs	675 g
1 t.	salt	5 mL
¼ t.	five spices powder	1 mL
¼ t.	black pepper	1 mL
1 t.	sugar	5 mL
1½ t.	soy sauce	7 mL
2 t.	sesame oil	10 mL
¼ t.	MSG (optional)	1 mL

Line 8 × 12-in. (20 × 30.5-cm) pan with aluminum foil. Cut spareribs into sections of 3 to 4 ribs; arrange in single layer on the foil. Mix together remaining ingredients; pour over spareribs and marinate at least 4 hours, turning once or twice so that all ribs are properly seasoned. Cover pan tightly with another piece of foil. Bake at 375 °F (190 °C) for 35 minutes. Uncover and bake 15 minutes. Turn ribs over and bake for another 15 minutes. Cut into bite-sized pieces. Leftover ribs can be frozen and reheated before serving. Serve hot or cold.

BAMBOO SHOOTS SOYBEAN SNACK

Bamboo Shoots Soybean Snack can be kept in the refrigerator for many months. It is rich in protein and vitamins and is a favorite snack for travellers.

1 lb.	dried soybeans	450 g
½ lb.	bamboo shoots or carrots, shredded	225 g
1 T.	salt	15 mL
¼ c.	soy sauce	60 mL
2 T.	sherry	30 mL
3 T.	sugar	45 mL

Soak soybeans in water until swollen, about 3 hours. Wash and rinse until soybeans are clean, then drain. Add 2 qt. (2 L) water; bring to a boil, lower heat and cook 1 hour. Add next 4 ingredients and simmer for 30 minutes; stir in the sugar and mix well. Spread evenly on a foil-lined cookie sheet. Bake at 300 °F (150 °C) for 30 minutes. Stir a couple of times during baking. Cool and store in airtight container.

LOTUS SANDWICH

½ lb.	lotus roots	225 g
½ lb.	ground beef	225 g
1 T.	preserved kohlrabi (tza tsai), chopped	15 mL
1 T.	scallion, chopped	15 mL
1 T.	cornstarch	15 mL
1 t.	salt	5 mL
½ t.	sugar	2 mL
⅛ t.	white pepper	.5 mL
1	egg	1
1 c.	all-purpose flour	250 mL
⅔ c.	water	180 mL
½–1 t.	salt, to taste	2–5 mL
½ t.	baking soda	2 mL
2 c.	vegetable oil	500 mL

Peel lotus roots, wash and cut into ¼-in. (6 mm) slices (20 slices). To make the filling, combine the next 7 ingredients and mix well; divide into 10 portions. Spread each filling portion between 2 pieces of lotus root. To make the batter, combine the remaining ingredients except the oil and mix well. Dip each sandwich into the batter. Heat the oil to 325 °F (165 °C); deep-fry until golden , about 5 minutes. Turn occasionally. Serve hot. Makes 10.

FRIED WON TONS

½ lb.	ground pork	225 g
2 c.	water chestnuts, chopped	500 mL
1½ t.	salt	7 mL
½ t.	sugar	2 mL
1–2 t.	sesame oil	5–10 mL
1 T.	scallion, chopped	15 mL
½ t.	fresh ginger, chopped	2 mL
¼ t.	MSG (optional)	1 mL
24	won ton wrappers	24
2 c.	peanut or vegetable oil	500 mL

Thoroughly mix the first 8 ingredients to make the filling. Place ½ to 1 t. (2 to 5 mL) filling in middle of each won ton wrapper. Fold over, pressing and sealing edges; then fold like a nurse's cap. The won tons are now ready to cook. To fry, heat oil to 375 °F (190 °C). Fry won tons 2 to 3 minutes or until golden brown. Serve hot. Makes 24.

WON TON SOUP

24	won tons	24
1 qt.	soup stock	1 L
1 c.	lettuce leaves, celery cabbage or any green leafy vegetable, shredded	250 mL
½ c.	leftover roast chicken, pork, or beef, shredded salt and black pepper to taste	125 mL
drops	sesame oil (optional) scallion, finely chopped, for garnish	drops

Prepare won tons as for Fried Won Tons until stuffed, but do not fry. Simmer won tons in boiling water for 3 minutes; drain and rinse under cold water. Bring stock to a boil; add vegetable and meat, bring to a boil, cooking until vegetable is tender, about 1 to 3 minutes. Add won tons to the soup; bring back to a boil and season to taste with salt and pepper. Serve hot, adding a few drops of sesame oil, if desired. Sprinkle with scallion.

DOW SA WON TON

豆砂云吞

Prepare the same as Fried Won Tons except use *dow sa* (black bean paste) as a filling. Deep-fry until golden brown. *Dow sa* is available at Chinese bakery shops. It can be kept in freezer for several months.

TARO ROOT SNACK

芋角

1 lb.	*taro roots*	*450 g*
⅓ c.	*wheat starch*	*90 mL*
⅔ c.	*boiling water*	*180 mL*
1½ t.	*salt*	*7 mL*
½ t.	*sugar*	*2 mL*
¼ t.	*five spices powder*	*1 mL*
2 T.	*vegetable oil*	*30 mL*
3	*Chinese dried mushrooms*	*3*
½ c.	*minced pork*	*125 mL*
1½ t.	*cornstarch*	*7 mL*
¼ t.	*sugar*	*1 mL*
½ t.	*salt*	*2 mL*
1 t.	*sherry*	*5 mL*
2 t.	*soy sauce*	*10 mL*
½ t.	*sesame oil*	*2 mL*
½ c.	*shrimps, chopped*	*125 mL*
2 t.	*cornstarch, mixed with 1 T. (15 mL) water*	*10 mL*
1 qt.	*vegetable oil for frying*	*1 L*
	all-purpose flour for rollling snacks	

Peel the taros and cut into thin slices. Place taro slices in a dish and steam over boiling water until soft, about 35 to 40 minutes. Mash well. Place wheat starch in a bowl; gradually add the boiling water, stirring until well blended. Add the mashed taro, salt, sugar, and spice; mix well and marinate in refrigerator for 2 hours. Rinse the mushrooms, cover with warm water until soft, about 30 minutes; drain and chop finely. Mix pork with the next 6 ingredients.

To cook, heat the oil in a wok. Add the mushrooms and stir-fry for a few seconds. Add the pork mixture, stirring for 1 minute. Add the shrimps and stir-fry 1 more minute. Stir in the diluted cornstarch and stir-fry until thickened. Remove from heat. Take about 3 T. (45 mL) of the taro and flatten into a circle about 3½ in. (8.9 cm); place 2 t. (10 mL) of the pork mixture in the middle. Bring the opposite sides together and shape the patty like a potato. Roll lightly in flour.

To fry, heat the oil to 350 °F (175 °C) and deep-fry until golden. Cooked taro snacks can be frozen. To reheat, thaw and bake at 375 °F (190 °C) or deep-fry again until crispy and golden brown. Serve hot (tastier) or cold.

PEKING SALAD (La Bai Tsai)

1 lb.	cabbage	450 g
½ lb.	cauliflower	225 g
2	carrots	2
10 slices	fresh ginger, shredded	10 slices
2–2½ T.	salt	30–37.5 mL
1 T.	sesame oil	15 mL
1 t.	anise peppercorns	5 mL
6 T.	vinegar	90 mL
¼ c.	sugar	60 mL
½–1 t.	red pepper flakes to taste or 1–2 fresh hot red peppers, shredded	2–5 mL

Cut cabbage and cauliflower into bite-sized pieces; slice carrots in thin pieces. Place vegetables and ginger in a colander; evenly sprinkle with the salt and marinate, tossing several times. Drain vegetables in a colander for 2 hours. Place marinated vegetables in a bowl; cover and refrigerate overnight.

To cook, heat oil in a wok over medium heat; add anise peppercorns, stirring until it browns and fragrance rises from the wok. Add vinegar and sugar; stir well and bring to a boil. Turn off heat and remove peppercorns; add red pepper flakes. Pour over the vegetables, mixing well; marinate for 2 hours. Pour liquid back into wok, bring to a boil, then pour over the salad; marinate 4 or more hours. Salad can be stored in refrigerator for several days. Serve warm or cool.

CANDIED WATER CHESTNUTS

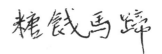

1 lb.	fresh water chestnuts	450 g
½ c.	sugar	125 mL
¼ c.	boiling water from water chestnuts	60 mL
1 t.	cornstarch mixed with 1 T. (15 mL) water	5 mL

Peel water chestnuts; cut in half, wash, and drain. Drop water chestnuts into 1 c. (250 mL) boiling water. Boil, stirring constantly, for 5 minutes; drain, saving ¼ c. (60 mL) of the cooking water. Mix sugar and the reserved cooking water; cook, stirring, until sugar dissolves. Add the dissolved cornstarch and mix well. Place cooked water chestnuts in the syrup and stir until each piece of water chestnut is coated.

Note: To make Candied Coconut Triangles, substitute fresh coconut for the water chestnuts. Prepare coconut meat by trimming off the brown skin and cutting coconut into small triangular pieces.

Tea —
the Everlasting Refreshment

Tea in the morning
Stimulates thinking, revives one's spirit.
Tea after meals
Clears the throat, helps digestion.
Tea during the bustle of day
Quenches thirst, does away with frustration.
Tea after work
Soothes the muscles, melts away fatigue.
Traditional Chinese tea-drinking song

Many dim sum dishes are traditionally served with tea. A meal begins with the choice of a tea that not only has its own distinct flavor but also reinforces and complements the delicate balance of the dim sum flavors without overpowering them.

The significance of tea in Chinese cultural life was established long ago. During the Tong Dynasty more than a thousand years ago, Lo Yu invented the process for manufacturing tea from the green or dried leaves of tea and other plants. Tea drinking as an art was seriously cultivated and became deeply woven into the lives and culture of the Chinese people.

Tea drinking began when herbal teas were brewed and consumed for medicinal purposes. Eventually, this practice developed social characteristics involving enjoyment and relaxing meditation. The Chinese people learned to appreciate tea drinking as an art of living and view it as a social function. By contrast, the Japanese believe the tea-drinking ritual to be a means of cultivating one's mind and character. The English believe tea drinking is invigorating and good for the body. Some Chinese tribal people—the Mongolians and Tibetans, for example, and some African desert people drink tea as a staple in their diet.

TYPES OF TEA

Most teas can be divided into three main categories:
1. *Fully fermented teas* include all types of red and black teas. Eighty percent of the world's tea belongs to this category, according to estimates. The most famous and

popular fully fermented Chinese teas are *chimen* or *keemun* (from Anhwei province), rose tea, and lychee black tea. The better quality red or black teas have small black or brown shrivelled leaves that brew into a deep red color and emit the fragrance of fruit mingled with burnt malt sugar. The leaves selected for these teas are picked from the young, tender, and smaller leaves of the plant.

2. *Partially fermented teas* include two types: *Oolong* tea (from Fukien or Taiwan), when brewed, develops into an orange-red color and has a ripened fruit bouquet; most Chinese restaurants serve this tea. *Bao tsung* tea provides an excellent base to combine with the aromatic and scented teas. When combining teas, the goal is to maintain a delicate balance between fragrance and flavor by blending three parts flower blossoms to seven parts tea leaves. The most widely known aromatic teas are jasmine (*shiang pien* or *mo-lee*), water nymph (*swee shien*), and sweet olive (*kwei hwa*). Jasmine is probably the most widely known scented tea in many countries. To vary its flavor, combine 1 teaspoon (5 mL) jasmine tea with the bud of a dried chrysanthemum. When brewed by itself, dried chrysanthemum, not a true tea, is quite bitter (although the taste can be improved by adding granulated or rock sugar). When dried chrysanthemum is added to jasmine tea, however, the mixture is not bitter and sweetening is unnecessary. The two flavors complement each other and produce a superior beverage.

3. *Nonfermented tea,* known as green tea, derives its flavor primarily from its plant sources and its growing seasons. When the leaves are freshly picked, they are immediately treated with a heat process to stop fermentation. They are then quickly dried. The final treatment prior to packaging is known as the "forming step." An excellent example of a nonfermented, green tea—gunpowder tea—has leaves that form curved, round balls, resembling gunpowder. When brewed with hot water, the balls open up and the whole leaf is revealed. Dragon well tea is another very popular green tea.

BREWING TEA

The best utensils for brewing and drinking tea are made of porcelain or pottery. Glass, plastic, or metal utensils change the natural flavor of the tea. All utensils used to make tea should be thoroughly cleaned.

Water is also very important in the brewing process. Many years ago, the water used to brew tea was rainwater or choice brook water flowing from famous springs. Waters from these sources are not conveniently obtainable today. Ideally, water to brew tea should have a low mineral content and the pot in which it is boiled should be odorless and without grease. Distilled or filtered soft tap water is preferred for tea brewing.

When making tea, the amount of tea per pot varies according to the type of tea and your desire for a stronger or weaker brew. As a general rule, use 1 teaspoon (5 mL) tea leaves for every cup (250 mL) water. To extract the finest fragrance and taste from the tea leaves, use water that has just come to a full boil. Normally, when more tea leaves are put into the pot with the addition of boiling water, the brewing time can be as short as two to three minutes. If only hot water is on hand, the brewing time should be increased to four to five minutes. The better quality tea leaves can be reused two or three times after the first brewing. A few special recipes for brewing tea with cold water are offered in this book. This method is not a traditional one, but the resulting brew provides a flavorful and refreshing version as well as convenient method because it can be prepared long before serving the tea.

Tea leaves will keep well and hold their fragrance and flavor when stored in air-tight, metal containers in a cool storage place. After each use, the tea container should be closed tightly to prevent moisture from seeping in. If the leaves do become slightly moist, they can be rejuvenated by placing them in a warm oven until they are thoroughly dried (be careful not to bake them). When tea is properly stored, age will not spoil its flavor and fragrance.

Tea drinking is still a popular cultural habit in China—a habit that has gradually spread to other countries for many reasons. Tea stimulates the palate and enhances the enjoyment of eating dim sum and other Chinese snacks by complementing the subtle blends of the ingredients. Even a brief interlude at the table with Chinese tea offers unique comfort and pleasure.

TEA GUIDE

TEA	PROVINCE/CITY	DESCRIPTION
Green		
Black dragon (*oolong*)	Taiwan	A cross between green and black tea; long, daintily tipped leaves; served at any time.
Cloud mist (*wun mo*)	Kiangsi	Generally served in the afternoon or at tea time; grown on high mountain cliffs; plucked and gathered by trained monkeys.
Dragon beard (*loong so*)	Canton	Also known as dragon's whiskers.
Dragon well (*jun jing*)	Chinkiang	One of the finest green teas; light in color, fresh in flavor.
Eyes of longevity (*sho may*)	Canton	Served between meals.
Fragrant petals (*heung peen*)	Chinkiang	Unusually fragrant; served at small parties for relatives or close friends.
Green tea (*lu an dow chow*)	Anhwei	Has the smell of newly mown hay.
Mulberry (*swong yuck*)	Hangchow	Made from young mulberry leaves.
Silver needle (*ngun jum*)	Canton	Served as a banquet tea.
Water nymph (*swee shien*)	Canton	A light tea, generally served in the midmorning.
Black		
Clear distance (*ching yuen*)	Canton	Preferable with evening snacks.
Iron goddess of mercy (*te kwan yin*)	Fukien	Quite thin, like a fine brandy; served in small cups. Grown on steep cliffs; gathered by monkeys.
Lapsang souchong	Yunan	Very smoky and strong.
poo nay	Yunan	Regarded as a powerful tonic.
su tang	Fukien	Generally served as an evening beverage.
wing chow	Canton	Breakfast tea.
woo lung	Chinkiang	Served at public teahouses with the talk of the day; smoky flavor.
Wu I	Yunan	Medicine for colds; very bitter.

Red

hung cha	Fukien	Served at teahouses and restaurants in the United States; dumped at the Boston Tea Party.
keemun	Kiangsi, Anhwei	Very popular; spicy, smooth, delicate; most famous.

Flower

Chrysanthemum (*chiu hwa*)	Chekiang	Sweetened with rock candy and served with Chinese pastry after meals.
Jasmine	Taiwan	Combination of dragon well leaves and flowers; aromatic, delicious.
mook lay fa	Fukien	
Lychee	Taiwan	Black tea with lychee leaf flavoring; faintly sweet.
lo cha	Taiwan	Combination of *oolong* and lychee flowers; served to renew friendship.
Rose (*mei kwei*)	Taiwan	Black tea with dried rosebuds.

ABOUT THE AUTHORS

The *Chinese Dessert, Dim Sum & Snack Cookbook* is the result of many years of enjoyment and preparation of Chinese dishes and dinners. The interaction of two couples—the Changs, by birth more representative of values of the East, and the Kutschers, of the West—has been instrumental in conceptualizing this effort.

The Changs have lived in many areas of the Far East, including Sumatra, Shanghai, Canton, and Hong Kong, and as children learned Chinese cooking from master chefs in the households of their parents. The Kutschers, Sinophiles and cooking enthusiasts, explored the excitement of Chinese cuisine from the vantage point of the American kitchen, and organized and shared their discoveries with those of the Changs.

The Changs, who met and married in China, settled in the United States in 1950 and became naturalized citizens. Wonona Chang was born in Sumatra and studied pediatrics in medical school in China until World War II. Currently, in addition to conducting cooking classes and food demonstrations, she teaches nursery school and continues her interest in music. She made the first recording in the U.S. of Chinese folk and art songs. Irving Chang, born in Kuling, China, was educated in China and continued graduate studies in the U.S. He is a chemist. The Changs live in Morristown, New Jersey.

The Kutschers are native New Yorkers. Austin Kutscher earned an undergraduate degree from New York University and a professional degree from Columbia University. He is a professor in the Department of Psychiatry, College of Physicians and Surgeons, and in the School of Dental and Oral Surgery at Columbia University. He is founder and president of the Foundation of Thanatology based at Columbia-Presbyterian Medical Center, New York. Lillian Kutscher, a graduate of Smith College, has edited 80 books on thanatology, directed to the health-science professions, for the Foundation of Thanatology. The Kutschers live in Scarsdale, New York.

These authors have shopped together to find the unique ingredients for their recipes, and then cooked together, challenged by the preparation of ethnic dishes to please many tastes. They have dined together in their own homes and in restaurants to critique their own creations and to discover what others might have to offer. They have become one family. The joys of their friendship have enriched their lives for more than twenty years and have provided the wellspring for this book, which they offer to add more pleasure to the lives of others.

INDEXES

Recipe Index

DESSERTS

DIM SUM & SNACKS

Index

orange/apricot, 52; rambutan/peach dessert tea, 54; real ginger ale, 49; rice wine, 57; soybean milk, 58; sparkling lychees with special flavors, 53; sweet rice wine, 57; sweet wine oranges, 53; triple delight iced tea with arbutus flavor, 55; water chestnut/peanut butter drink, 49; water chestnut/sesame butter drink, 57

Black bean paste: glutinous (sweet rice) cake, 33; New Year dumplings with, 113; sesame balls, 118; won ton, 140

Blackberry: punch, lychee with ginger flavor, 51

Black cherry: lychees, 83; plum punch, 52

Bok tsoi, 13–14

Boysenberry: yogurt with Chinese flavors, 97

Brands of ingredients, 11

Bread dough, Chinese, 119

Brown sugar, 11

Butter: ginger spread, 106

C

Cabbage, white Chinese, 13–14

Cake: almond pound, 29; Aunt Dot's Nien Gao, 115; banana, 29; Cantonese steamed, 27; date nut squares, 31; doughnut slices with Chinese flavors, 33; fresh ginger zucchini carrot, 28–29; ginger jam jelly roll, 32; ginger marmalade pudding, 95; glutinous (sweet rice), 33; golden nut, 33; longan "dragon eye" banana, 28; luscious lime squares, 30; meringue shells, 34; New Year, 117; nine layered, 117; noodle, 32; prune, 30; pudding, ginger lemon, 94; red bean, 27; steamed carrot, 28; sweet olive New Year, 116; turnip, 116–117; walnut torte, 34; white sweet steamed, 116; yummy yam, 31

Champagne: lychee/raspberry medley in, 85

Candied: pomelo or grapefruit, 118; walnuts, 48; water chestnuts, 141

Candies (See Confections)

Cantaloupe: with two Chinese flavors, 80

Cantonese, 8; chow mein, 126; lychees, 83; steamed egg, 127

Carrot: cake, fresh ginger zucchini, 28–29; steamed cake, 28

Cashew: roasted, 47

Cellophane noodles, 20

Champagne: lychee snow, 68

Cha-shu; bao tzu: baked, 120–121; lo mein, 123

Cherry. (See also Black cherry): lychee pie, 42; maraschino sauce, rambutans in, 105; in plum wine, 87; rambutan/loquat punch, 52

Chestnut, water. (See Water chestnut)

Chicken: curried rice noodles, 124; drunken, 125; lo mein, shredded, 123; mushroom bao tzu, 120; rolls, 125

Chinese apple, 8

Chinese flavors. (See also specific flavors): doughnut slices with, 33

Chocolate: dipped fortune cookies, 46; dipped lychees, 46

Chow mein: Cantonese, 126

Coconut: glutinous rice balls, 114; ice cream, simple, 61; ice cream, simple strawberry, 64; kisses, 46; strips, Chinese, 14

Compote: arbutus, 76; chilled ginger/pineapple, 78; hot lychee, 76; Chinese fruit cocktail, 75; combinations for, 22–23; ginger fruit, 75; hot Chinese, 74; li-ly, 78; loquat, 78; mandarin orange/melba, 77

Confections: apricot-kumquat balls, 43; apricots stuffed with ginger, 44; chocolate-dipped fortune cookies, 46; chocolate-dipped lychees, 46; coconut kisses, 46; eleven precious ingredients stuffed lychees, 43; frosted lychees, 44; honey-dipped glazed fruits stuffed with oriental delights, 45; natural dried fruits stuffed with oriental delights, 45; orange sesame strips, 44; oriental almond gel candy, 46; yam or sweet potato toffee, 44

Conserve: ginger/apple dessert, 82

Cointreau liqueur: ice cream, 61

Conversion guides, 10

Cookie: almond, 14; almond dream bars, 37; anise, 35; coconut-fruit-nut bars, 36; fortune, chocolate-dipped, 46; ice cream sandwiches, almond, 68; pine-nuts almond, 36; sesame, 35

Cranberry: mandarin orange sauce, hot, 102

Cream cheese: ginger topping, 109

Cream: frozen almond honey, 92; lychee tapioca, 93

Crepe: scallion, 137

Cucumber, white preserved: as stuffing for natural dried fruits, 45; honey-dipped glazed fruits stuffed with, 45

Curried: chicken rice noodles, 124; jao filling, 124

Custard: base for ice cream, 60; lychee tofu, 91; peach tofu, 93; soft egg with plum wine, 95; sweet rice wine egg, 94; tarts, almond, 41

D

Date jam, 14–15; as stuffing for natural dried fruits, 45; Chinese whip, 100; doughnut slices with Chinese flavors, 33; flavor, Chinese with baked tangerines, 72; flavor, with baked apples, 71; flavor, with baked grapefruit, 72; honey-dipped glazed fruits stuffed with, 45; ice cream, 61; strawberries, 80; tofu sauce, 101; topping, 107

Dates, red, dried, 15

hot compote, 76; ice, 66; ice cream, 62; ice cream, simple, 62; ice cream, simple banana, 62; ice cubes, 55; jasmine tea, 54; jasmine/tea punch, 55; lemon sauce, 104; li-ly compote, 78; li-ly punch, 53; liqueur compote, 76; longan/mandarin orange gel dessert, 98; longan/mandarin orange nectar, 50; loquat/mandarin orange/strawberry punch, 50–51; lychee black tea, 53; Mandarine Napoléon liqueur glaze, 110; mandarin orange/strawberry punch, 51; marshmallow frosting, 109; melba punch, 51; melba sauce, 103; peach frosted, 56; peachy preserves, 89; peach tofu cooler, 56; punch, five different ingredient, 51; raspberry medley in champagne, 85; ring, 99; sauce, 102; shake, 56; sherbet, 66; sparkling with special flavors, 53; special-flavored Chinese fruit and, 81; specially sweet aromatic, 83; stuffed, eleven precious ingredients, 43; sugar cane drink with ginger flavor, 49; tapioca cream, 93; tofu custard, 91; whip, 100

M

Mandarine Napoléon liqueur, 18: baked lychees with, 72; honey/ginger topping, 108; kumquat topping, 108; longan sauce, 104; lychee compote, 76; lychee glaze, 110; marshmallow topping with, 108; with banana fritters, 38

Mandarin oranges, 19; and strawberries with Chinese liqueur, 86; ambrosia, 69; dessert gel/sauce, 108; hot cranberry sauce, 102; ice cream, 63; in wine and liqueur, 86; kumquat, 78; longan ice, 67; longan tofu, 91; lychee/longan gel dessert, 98; lychee/longan nectar, 50; lychee/loquat/strawberry punch, 50–51; melba compote, 77; peach freeze whip, 66; peaches, 82; pineapple sherbet, 66; punch, five different ingredient, 51; punch, lychee/strawberry, 51; rambutan/apricot drink, 52; sherbet, 66; snow, 67; soufflé, 92; sugar cane fruit drink, 49; swizzle, 57; with ginger, 82; with tofu, 93; yogurt, 97

Mango, 19: ice cream, 62; sherbet, 65

Marmalade: ginger/orange, 88; ginger with lychees, 90; orange/real ginger, 89; oriental spiked, 89; oriental with orange flavor, 89

Marshmallow: almond whip, 68; ginger topping, 107; lychee frosting, 109; topping with kumquats, 108; topping with liqueur, 108

Measurements, equivalent, 10

Meatballs: pearl, 129

Mélange: lychee/cherry, 82

Melba: lychee sauce, 103; mandarin orange compote, 77

Melon: frozen balls/loquat in melon cordial, 85; seeds, 19; winter, 19

Melon liqueur: ice cream, 63; loquat/frozen melon balls in, 85

Milk: soybean, 58; soybean dessert, 97

Mousse: peanut, 92

Mung bean: sweet soup, 121

Mushroom: chicken bao tzu, 120; dried Chinese, 20

Mustard greens: hot or szechwan chung tsai, 135

N

Nectar: lychee/longan/mandarin orange, 50

Nectarine: Chinese stir-fried, 73; with kumquat flavor, 80

New Year: cake, 8, 117; dumplings with peanut butter, 113; dumplings with sweet black bean paste, 113; dumplings with sweet rice wine, 113; sweet olive cake, 116

New Year's Eve festival (*Tuan Nien*), 8

Noodles: cake, 32; instant, 133; instant with soup, 133

Noodles, cellophane, 20

Noodles, fresh, 20

Noodles, rice: curried chicken, 124

Nut: Angela's sugar and spice, 125; bars, coconut-fruit-, 36; candied walnuts, 48; date squares, 31; five spices sweet-salty peanuts, 48; five spices unsalted peanuts, 48; glazed almonds, 47; golden cake, 33; lychee/apricot squares, 30–31; pistachio ice cream, 63; roasted cashews, 47; roasted peanuts, 47; walnut strips, 48; walnut torte, 34

O

Orange: flavor, oriental marmalade with, 89; sesame strips, 44; sweet wine, 53

Orange marmalade: ginger preserves, 88; sauce, 104; tofu icing, 107

P

Pancake. (*See also* Crepe): banana, 39; bo bing, 122; fried bean paste, 40; scallion, 137

Parfait: almond, 64; Chinese fruit slush, 68

Pastry: almond custard tarts, 41; lychee/cherry pie, 42; sweet piecrust, 42; white peach tarts, 41

Peach: almond, 83; almond ice cream, 60; dessert/tea, rambutan, 54; gingered, 79; ginger ice cream, 61; ginger yogurt, 96; ice cream, 63; lychee frosted, 56; lychee tofu cooler, 56; mandarin orange, 82; preserves, lychee, 89; punch, ginger, 51; tofu custard, 93

Peanut butter: cream topping, 107; drink, water chestnut, 49; glutinous rice balls with, 114; New Year dumplings with, 113; sauce, 104–105

lychee, 66; mandarin orange, 66; mandarin orange/pineapple, 66; mango, 65

Shou Swei, 8

Shrimp: anise pepper-salt ball, 131; dried, 21; fried dumplings, 128–129; go-te, 130; Joan's fluffy, 135; toast, 135

Snacks, 7; recipe section, 113–141

Snow: ginger, 67; lychee champagne, 68; mandarin orange, 67

So, 8

Soufflé: mandarin orange, 92

Soup: instant noodles with, 133; mung bean, 121; won ton, 139

Soybean: bamboo shoots snack, 138; milk, 58; milk dessert, 97

Spareribs: with special sauce, 138; steamed, 138

Spread. (*See also* Topping): ginger butter, 106; ginger sweet red bean dessert, 106; kumquat frosting, 110

Squares. (*See* Cooky)

Steamed: Cantonese cake, 27; Cantonese egg, 127; carrot cake, 28; rice rolls, 134–135; spareribs, 138; white sweet cake, 116

Stir-fried: nectarine, Chinese, 73; strawberries with kumquat, 73

Strawberry: ambrosia, 70; and mandarin oranges with Chinese liqueur, 86; Chinese stir-fried with kumquat, 73; dated, 80; five different ingredient, 51; longan gelatin, 100; lychee/loquat/mandarin orange punch, 50–51; punch, lychee/mandarin orange, 51; tofu pudding, 91

Stuffing: for natural dried fruits, Chinese preserved foods as, 45

Suey gow: beef, 130–131; wrappers, 130

Sugar cane, 8; drink, lychee with ginger flavor, 49; fruit drink, mandarin orange, 49; pineapple punch, 52

Sugar cane drink, 21

Sweet potato: or yam toffee, 44

Sweet and sour: lotus root, 129

Syrup: ginger sugar, 109; plum wine, 105

T

Tangerine, 8. (*See also* Mandarin orange): baked with Chinese date flavor, 72

Tapioca: longan pudding, 94; lychee cream, 93; pineapple, 95

Taro root: snack, 140

Tart: almond custard, 41; white peach, 41

Tea, 8: black, lychee/lychee, 53; brewing of, 143–144; Chinese iced jasmine, 54; egg, five spices, 126; fourteen precious ingredients, 54; fruit for dessert, 53; guide, 144–145; jasmine lychee, 54; keemun, with lychee flavor, 56;

punch, jasmine/lychee, 55; rambutan/peach dessert, 54; rose, iced, 56; rose, iced with loquat flavor, 56; significance in Chinese culture, 142; triple delight iced with arbutus flavor, 55; types, 142–143

Toast: shrimp, 135

Toffee: yam or sweet potato, 44

Tofu (bean curd; dow foo), 13: cooler, lychee peach, 56; longan/mandarin orange, 91; mandarin oranges with, 93; orange icing, 107; peach custard, 93; strawberry pudding, 91

Topping, 23. (*See also* Spread); almond, 107; almond lychee glaze, 107; date jam, 107; frozen lychee fluff, 106; ginger, 108; ginger cream, 109; ginger cream cheese, 109; ginger whipped, 109; honey/ginger Mandarine Napoléon liqueur, 108; kumquat liqueur, 108; marshmallow ginger, 107; marshmallow with liqueur, 108; peanut cream, 107; two ginger, 108

Trifle: lychee, 95

Tuan Nien, 8

Turnip: cake, 116–117

U

Utensils, 11

V

Vanilla: ice cream, 60

W

Walnut: candied, 48; strips, 48; torte, 34

Wan nien liang, 8

Water chestnut, 15: candied, 141; peanut butter drink, 49; sesame butter drink, 57

Watermelon seed, 8

Whip: almond marshmallow, 68; Chinese date, 100; longan, 99; lychee, 100; lychee lemon ice, 97

Wine: and liqueur, mandarin oranges in, 86; oranges, sweet, 53; rice, 57

Won ton: *dow sa*, 140; fried, 139; soup, 139

Wrappers: curried jao, 124; go-te or suey gow, 130; har gow, 132; shu mai, 136

Y

Yam: cake, yummy, 31; or sweet potato toffee, 44

Yogurt: almond-flavored, 97; almond/orange marmalade, 97; boysenberry, with Chinese flavors, 97; ginger, 100 mandarin orange, 97; peachy ginger, 96